T0385222

terrain

THE HOUSE PLANT BOOK

terrain

THE HOUSE PLANT BOOK

An Insider's Guide to
Cultivating and Collecting
the Most Sought-After
Specimens

Melissa Lowrie and the TERRAIN plant team

Words by Caroline Lees

Principal photography by Kate Jordan

ARTISAN | NEW YORK

Library of Congress Cataloging-in-Publication Data

Names: Lowrie, Melissa, author. | Lees, Caroline, author. | Jordan, Kate S., photographer.
Title: Terrain: the houseplant book : an insider's guide to cultivating and collecting the most sought-after specimens / Melissa Lowrie and the Terrain plant team ; words by Caroline Lees, photography by Kate Jordan
Description: New York : Artisan, [2022]
Identifiers: LCCN 2022010977 | ISBN 9781648290909
Subjects: LCSH: House plants. | Indoor gardening. | Handbooks and manuals.
Classification: LCC SB419 .L69 2022 | DDC 635.9/65—dc23/eng/20220316
LC record available at https://lccn.loc.gov/2022010977

Design by Toni Tajima

Artisan books are available at special discounts when purchased in bulk for premiums and sales promotions as well as for fund-raising or educational use. Special editions or book excerpts also can be created to specification. For details, contact the Special Sales Director at the address below, or send an e-mail to specialmarkets@workman.com.

For speaking engagements, contact speakersbureau@workman.com.

Published by Artisan
A division of Workman Publishing Co., Inc.
225 Varick Street
New York, NY 10014-4381
artisanbooks.com

Artisan is a registered trademark of Workman Publishing Co., Inc.

Printed in China on responsibly sourced paper
First printing, September 2022

10 9 8 7 6 5 4 3 2 1

CONTENTS

INTRODUCTION

I CAME TO PLANTS the way I suspect many of us do—through my mom. I grew up walking her gardens ritualistically. We toured the new spring growth together as the days warmed. When summer arrived, we harvested produce early in the morning before the heat of the day set in. After fall brought about the end of the growing season, we spent winter poring over seed catalogs and planning next year's plantings.

For me, and for many plant people, this ebb and flow of the seasons grounds us in nature. Though it's subtler, houseplants have a seasonality, too. Most slow their growth in winter when the days are short, conserving energy until spring, when the hours of sunlight lengthen and growth begins again. When we bring plants indoors, we are able to observe these cycles of growth in close proximity. Tending to houseplants is a practice in mindfulness; there's a meditative quality to making daily rounds to observe a slowly unfurling fern frond, mist plants, or prune spent leaves.

I joined Terrain as a plant buyer before the brand's launch in 2008, alongside a team of like-minded people who loved the natural world. Our aim was to reimagine the local garden center as a celebration of both seasonality and our customers' self-expression, through the lens of living with nature indoors and out. We set out to explore the many ways people think about plants in the spaces they inhabit, starting with a houseplant selection that highlighted the simple beauty of familiar forms. When we opened our doors, we were focused on elevating time-honored plants like maidenhair ferns and overgrown heirloom begonias in mossy pots while prioritizing specialty growers and collectible varieties to cultivate a diverse inventory of unexpected statement pieces.

In those early days, the fiddle-leaf fig was still a few years away from galvanizing the demand for "aspirational" plants (though we were already falling for its form). Its meteoric rise, along with the surge of houseplant content on Pinterest and Instagram, spurred a never-ending pursuit of the next perfect plant. Terrain found new customers eager to possess the "fashionable" specimens they saw online. This shift was just one of myriad changes in the plant industry during this time; it forced many growers to reevaluate rules they had followed for decades, adjust what they were growing, and pivot to new retail channels including online sales.

When I started working with plants in the late 1990s, I was usually the youngest person in the room, and often one of very few women. Many farms were small multigenerational family operations, often without a successor to continue the business. By the time the houseplant trend exploded, lots of these farms had been bought by big-box suppliers or the medical marijuana industry. Those remaining had spent years growing large quantities of more common plants but were not yet investing in specialty areas. So when demand for trendy and specialty plants approached fever pitch, supply couldn't keep up. As we entered the 2020s, houseplants saw another boom on top of the existing wave of popularity, when we all slowed down and spent more time at home. Just as growers were catching up with the market, it doubled in size.

With such unprecedented interest, Terrain's deep relationships with our growers have been vital to our ability to create a dynamic assortment and maintain availability for the most in-demand houseplants. The plant industry is incredibly decentralized; there's no overarching system for understanding what exists in any one region, so the best way to source plants is to go out and find them.

Grower visits have always been my favorite part of my job. Plant people are, by and large, really special humans, and I've been lucky to have many of them as unofficial teachers during my horticultural journey. Each visit is an opportunity to learn more about the plants, their cultivation, and how they grow. I love asking growers what they're excited about, seeing what they're tinkering with in the back of the greenhouse, or nerding out with them over new cultivars and exciting mutations. These relationships are also important because they provide me with a deeper understanding of how growers source and propagate their plants, which is especially important given the current state of the industry. As demand for rare plants increases, ethical growing and stewardship of native habitats are more crucial than ever. Recently, these visits have also become a chance to meet the next generation of growers. Since the houseplant boom began, many millennials and Gen Zers are choosing to stay in the family business, infusing the industry with a younger, more diverse demographic. To give you a window into these experiences, this book includes visits to some of my favorite growers, offering a peek inside their worlds.

The book's organization—with plants grouped by botanical family, habit or commonalities in care, or design possibilities—reflects my plant buyer brain, and can help to inform where you might place them and how you might plant or care for them. Within each grouping, you'll find profiles showcasing a single cultivar or genus, plus specimen guides that dive deeper into a category or genus to demonstrate how vastly varied even close relatives within the plant kingdom can be.

Whether you found your way to houseplants in recent years or are a decades-long devotee, I hope that this book offers you not only a greater understanding of how to choose and care for plants but also a deeper appreciation of their magical details. The photographs accompanying each profile highlight intricate veins, tiny hairs, and the plant world's wealth of textures. You'll also notice imperfections—and that's on purpose. Plants are unpredictable and always transforming; wildly shaped weirdos hold as much beauty as perfectly pruned specimens. Another note on photography: Much of the joy of living with houseplants is experiencing the way that these beings interact with and change the light in your

PREVIOUS PAGES, LEFT: The hothouse at Terrain's flagship store in Glen Mills, Pennsylvania, around the time of the store's opening in 2008. OPPOSITE: A selection of ferns in the shade house at the same Terrain location in 2022.

spaces. To that end, the images that open each chapter play upon the idea of plants and shadows in the home.

Along with a look at some exceptional plants, I want to give you permission to try, make mistakes, learn, and try again! Don't be discouraged if you don't get something right the first time. Keeping plants in your home is a long game, but the rewards are sublime. Throughout the seasons, they delight the senses, teach patience and curiosity, and offer endless surprise as companions both outdoors and in.

CARING FOR HOUSEPLANTS

THIS GUIDE WILL, of course, cover care essentials like water, light, and soil. But the most important thing you can give your plants is your presence. Patience and observation are as important as action when it comes to plant care, so get to know the green, growing members of your household. Study your plant's color and texture when it's watered and when it's dry; notice when it receives light throughout the day and how much; turn the leaves over to understand how clean, healthy foliage looks. Many houseplants don't want a lot of fuss, but some need it to thrive. You'll never know what is required, however, unless you invest the time to develop a deep familiarity. Keep your plant near so you have the opportunity to notice its every change. This intimate relationship is one of the great joys of caring for houseplants.

To build a strong foundation for the relationship between you and your houseplants, start by understanding their origins. A plant's native habitat informs how it should be cared for at home and the ways you may have to compensate for what your home lacks. Tropical plants, for example, want high humidity, uniform moisture, warm temperatures, and consistent light. Desert plants are sensitive to overwatering but can tolerate temperature swings that would challenge more tender forest-native species. Knowing this background can help you give your houseplants more of what they need to thrive—which is why we've included details about each plant's origins in the profiles in this book.

POTS & STRUCTURES

When you bring home a new houseplant, give it space and support to grow by choosing the right pot or, in the case of some vining plants, the right pairing of pot and structure.

Pots

Pick your growing pot based on your plant's watering requirements and size. A houseplant that prefers drier soil is best suited to a pot made of a raw, unglazed material (such as terra-cotta or clay), which will wick water away from the soil (this also makes porous, unglazed pots a good choice if you tend to be heavy-handed when watering). Plants that need consistent moisture should be placed in plastic or glazed ceramic pots; nonporous materials keep soil wetter longer. All growing pots should have drainage holes to prevent water from pooling near the roots, which can cause rot and disease. Pair your pot with a saucer or tray to protect indoor surfaces.

Keep pot shape in mind, too. In general, vessels have four basic silhouettes: tapered,

straight-sided, inward-curved, and elevated (like an urn). Tapered pots are best for plants prone to root rot or waterlogging; the design encourages evaporation, helping the soil dry between waterings. Straight-sided and inward-curved containers cause slower evaporation, so are good for plants that prefer more moisture. Urns elevate plants with cascading or pendulous habits. There are, of course, shapes beyond these basics. Consider a low bowl for plants with shallow root systems or rhizomes, like footed ferns and begonias. Hanging baskets are well suited to cascading plants, but those without drainage can retain excess water; we suggest a hanging apparatus that can hold a pot with a drainage hole and a saucer. Throughout our plant profiles, we've called out when a particular pot shape is most suitable.

Once you've determined the right material and shape, select a pot that's only slightly larger than the plant's current root-ball. You can always move the plant to a larger pot as it grows (see page 30), but starting with too large a pot can kill a plant if it doesn't have an expansive enough root system to use all the water that the soil can hold.

Growing pots must be selected based on a plant's needs, but to suit your aesthetic preferences, you may choose to disguise the plastic grower's pot that comes home with your plant from the nursery by pairing it with a cachepot. Cachepots are decorative containers without drainage holes. A grower's pot can be placed inside, and it should slip in and out easily for watering or other maintenance.

Structures

Vining plants that have a tendency to climb need support. Without the aid of a structure, they will break under their own weight, become an unhappy mess on the floor, or attempt to navigate your furniture as they reach for the sky.

Some plants—including dischidia (page 179), climbing rock plant (page 222), and angel vine (page 185)—can be trained to grow on many types of structures. There are lots of ready-made options; common shapes include hoops, obelisks, tuteurs, bamboo tripods, and trellises. Other plants prefer organic materials like moss poles (see right) or wood supports. For smaller or lighter specimens, you can simply use a piece of wire bent into the desired shape. You can also make a basic structure using heavy-gauge wire or bamboo poles; or utilize an existing support in your home, such as an unheated pipe or the side of a bookshelf.

Once you've selected the structure, you'll need to train the plant onto it. Smaller plants (like the angel vine shown here) don't need anything to adhere them to a support. Just gently and loosely wrap individual tendrils around the structure, encouraging them to grow upon it. For more substantial specimens, attach stems using bind wire, garden twine, or Velcro plant ties. Anchor the stem at intervals, using the fewest attachments possible. Don't tie too tightly—the plant needs room to expand within the tie and along the structure.

Plants with aerial roots, like aroids, will eventually stabilize themselves and no longer need anchors. More delicate vines, like hoyas and angel vines, will continue to produce new tendrils that you'll want to encourage toward your desired shape. As offshoots emerge, decide whether to wrap them around the structure or let them explore freely.

MOSS POLES

Climbers with aerial roots, like monsteras (page 53), philodendrons (page 42), and vining aroids (page 54), prefer a moss pole that mimics their native support: the nooks and crannies of a tree. These plants will especially appreciate the moss pole's many points of attachment and constant supply of moisture. Premade moss poles are widely available for purchase.

SOIL

The purpose of a growing medium is to supply a plant with nutrients, manage water drainage and airflow, and provide structure for roots to anchor the plant in its pot. Though often referred to as "soil," many growing mediums are actually soilless mixes. Typically composed with a base of peat or coconut coir, these mixes have more drainage elements than soil and are fully sterile. Custom-blended potting mixes are available to meet the needs of many houseplant types. In the plant profiles that follow, we recommend four basic types of commercially available mixes:

1. **Potting Mix.** A light and sterile soilless blend—often a base of peat moss or coconut coir mixed with perlite, sometimes with vermiculite and pine bark—that has the general nutrition, water retention, and drainage properties required by many houseplants. In most situations, blends labeled "houseplant mixes" can be used interchangeably with potting mix. Mixes billed as "moisture retaining" often have crystals or gel components to increase water retention—be cautious, as this can sometimes complicate plant care by causing uneven water evaporation.

2. **Succulent Mix.** A heavy, porous, well-draining mix of coarse aggregates that's optimal for succulents. Component parts may include gravel, coarse sand, some organic matter, and/or baked clay products.

3. **African Violet Mix.** A lightweight, moisture-retaining soilless mix containing micronutrients specifically for African violets and other gesneriads.

4. **Orchid Mix.** This soilless, chunky mix can hold moisture if well saturated, but it is well draining and has a larger aggregate size for plants that need structure in their substrate,

like orchids and many epiphytes. It typically contains a blend of pine bark and other aggregates, such as sphagnum moss, perlite, expanded clay, charcoal, coconut husk chips, pumice, and lava rock.

POTTING MIX VS POTTING SOIL

Commercially available potting *soil* differs from potting *mix*; the former is a heavier blend that often contains garden soil, sand, and compost and is not sterile, meaning it could harbor fungi, disease, and even stray seeds. As such, potting soil and garden soil are not recommended for houseplants.

Amended Mixes & Custom Blends

Once you understand the different elements of a growing substrate, you may want to tailor mixes specifically to your individual houseplants. The simplest way to make a custom blend is to begin with a high-quality potting mix and amend it to suit a plant's nutrient, water retention, and structural needs (more on this to follow). We've noted how you might want to amend your mixes where applicable in our plant profiles. For best results, always start with presterilized components from a reputable source.

As you get more comfortable with this and see the benefit of your modifications, you might choose to make your own blends from scratch. There are many homemade potting mix recipes to reference online; most recommend a base of peat moss or well-washed coconut coir in a 60:40 ratio to drainage substrates like perlite, vermiculite, or fine orchid bark. To this basic recipe, other drainage and nutritional components can be added to further customize the mix and support a plant's particular needs.

NUTRITION

All plants need nutrients to grow. Nitrogen, phosphorus, potassium, sulfur, calcium, and magnesium are macronutrients that plants generally need in larger quantities. Micronutrients comprise all other nutrients and are just as necessary for plant health; plants simply need them in smaller quantities. Plants that require nutrient-rich soil need a mix that provides both macro- and micronutrients. You can build nutrients into your soil using the four amendments below. Adding a slow-release fertilizer at the time of planting is optional but highly recommended (see Fertilizer, page 24, for additional information on plant nutrition).

1. **Compost.** A soilless component made of well-rotted organic matter, compost is an excellent source of nutrients and a great addition to a custom mix for plants that need loamy, nutrient-rich soil. Note: For indoor use, compost must be sterilized (in other words, you will need to purchase it, rather than making it yourself).

2. **Biochar.** A porous charcoal product, biochar is a stable form of carbon that improves soil quality while delivering macronutrients to roots, promoting microbial activity, and regulating the leaching of nitrogen and other nutrients from the soil. It's best used in conjunction with compost and other organic nutrients.

3. **Worm Castings.** Worm "poop," or vermicast, has gained popularity as an excellent source of nutritional content for plants. It fortifies soil blends with micronutrients and trace elements that help plants thrive.

4. **Humus.** Like compost, humus is well-rotted organic matter. However, it forms over longer periods of time and is mostly made of carbon (compost contains carbon as well as other nutrients). Humus is typically found in garden soils. Humans compost; nature makes humus.

DRAINAGE, AERATION & WEIGHT

The component parts of a soil or soilless mix affect how well that mix retains or sheds excess water (drainage), as well as how much air space it provides for roots to grow and exchange gases (aeration). All mixes must support these two functions while also supplying water and nutrients to roots.

The size of a mix's component parts is called aggregate size, and this size affects both the soil's drainage and aeration. Aggregate size can be chunky (think small wood chips) or fine (like sawdust—but don't use sawdust!). A coarse, chunky, or larger aggregate mix provides lots of space for roots to grow and water to run through, while fine mixes are denser and retain water better. All the components of a mix should be about the same size, as varied sizes can lead to waterlogging.

The plant's need for water retention should also be considered, as different soilless components vary in their capacity to hold and release moisture. Gravel and stone have no capacity to hold moisture and are helpful for arid, well-draining mixes. Barks, vermiculite, and perlite absorb water and release it slowly as the surrounding mix dries, so they are useful for plants that need moderate to high water retention.

Along with your plant's drainage and aeration needs, you'll want to consider its physical needs. Different aggregates have different weight properties; heavier blends can balance the physical weight of top-heavy plants like cane begonias (page 93) or larger succulents, while lighter mixes typically contain less compost or soil components and may not support a heavy plant. For more on these options, turn the page.

11 COMMON AGGREGATES

Here are some basic components used to build custom potting mixes:

1. **Peat Moss.** A soilless component made of organic matter that has decomposed under anaerobic (oxygen-free) conditions specific to swamps and bogs, peat is lightweight, very finely textured, and retains moisture well. It's also a great acidifier. However, peat can be challenging to rehydrate if it becomes too dry, and there are ongoing conversations about its sustainability (see opposite).

2. **Coconut Coir.** A lightweight, soilless component made of shredded coconut husk fibers, coconut coir is an alternative to peat as a potting mix base: it retains water well, needs less water to saturate, has a relatively neutral pH, and doesn't compress. However, coconut coir lacks some of the micronutrient benefits found in peat, and must be rinsed well to remove trace salts from the harvesting process.

3. **Coconut Husk.** Made from chipped coconut shells, coconut husk closely resembles a fine mulch and aids in absorbing and releasing

water while adding aeration. It's frequently found in orchid mixes.

4. Pumice. A porous volcanic by-product, pumice is similar to perlite (see below) but often slightly coarser in texture. Pumice adds aeration to mixes but is heavier than perlite and won't rise to the top of the soil.

5. Bark Nuggets. The main ingredient in most orchid mixes, bark nuggets are primarily made of pine bark. They come in a range of particle sizes and textures, providing a straightforward way to customize the texture of a mix to a plant's needs while providing aeration and structure.

6. Rice Hulls. A lightweight by-product of rice production, rice hulls are a sustainable option for improving soil aeration and drainage. Rice hulls are lightweight and have good water retention.

7. Perlite. A volcanic mineral superheated to "puff" into small white aggregates, perlite is used to improve soil texture and retains both water and air (unlike vermiculite; see below). It's very lightweight and will float to the top of a mix—a look we prefer to avoid.

8. Vermiculite. Mica that's been superheated to become "spongy" and lightweight, vermiculite is used to improve soil texture while retaining moisture that can be slowly released back to plants as they need it. It's finely textured and best used in mixes for water-loving plants.

9. Calcined Clay. A baked clay product, calcined clay is typically heavy and coarse, and absorbs and slowly releases excess water and nutrients. It also functions as an acidifier. Excellent for top-heavy plants that need even, semidry conditions.

10. Sand. Commercially available sand ranges from play and beach sand to coarser, heavier aggregates. Only coarse sand should be used as a soil amendment, as play/beach sand is too fine and will clog the soil's air spaces, leading to waterlogging.

11. Charcoal. Sometimes used as a drainage filler for coarse mixes, horticultural charcoal is a lightweight amendment with the texture of fine mulch. It can be helpful in lowering the pH of the mix and providing some level of filtering for impurities in water.

A NOTE ON SUSTAINABILITY

Consider sustainability when choosing a growing medium. There is an ongoing and complicated global conversation around peat; while some countries are making headway toward sustainable peat farming, peat is a natural resource and peat mining contributes significantly to global CO_2 emission levels. Coconut coir is readily available as a by-product of coconut farming, but there are concerns around the ecological impact of its processing, which requires large amounts of water. Innovators are pioneering peat- and coir-free potting mixes that prioritize sustainability, so look for options with these factors in mind while the industry works toward sustainable solutions.

LIGHT

Light can be quantified in two ways: duration and intensity. Duration is the amount of light each day, which controls a plant's internal clock. Longer days signal spring or summer—time to grow (more hours of light mean more time to photosynthesize). Fewer hours of light signal the transition to fall and winter and may induce a resting period of less growth and minimal to no flowering. In general, plants want twelve to sixteen hours of light each day to grow and flower. When resting, they can tolerate less, but no fewer than eight hours per day.

Intensity is the quality of light, and it represents the energy the light holds. An equatorial mountaintop in full summer sun would have the most energy-filled light on Earth, while a dim hallway offers very little. Some plants have evolved to absorb and process lots of light energy; these are typically big, rapid growers or profuse bloomers. Other plants are adapted to make the most of less light and get overwhelmed by higher intensity (among these, you'll find some of our favorite houseplants for filling niches throughout the home). Understanding a plant's native habitat can help you match it to the right light conditions. Does it grow in the shady forest understory? Does it bake below the desert sun? All plants need light energy, but where they should reside in relation to the windows in your home is dictated by their preferred intensity.

BRIGHT DIRECT-LIGHT PLANTS need full sun and should be as close to a window as possible. (Keep in mind that light intensity diminishes by about 95 percent within a few feet/0.9 m of a window.) In the Northern Hemisphere, the window should be south-facing and unobstructed.

BRIGHT INDIRECT-LIGHT PLANTS should be just outside the range of direct sunlight from a southern window (2 to 3 feet/0.6 to 0.9 m), or very close to an east- or west-facing window. They do not tolerate direct sun on their leaves for very long (if at all) and never in the afternoon. In nature, they live under the filter of an open canopy or at the forest edge.

MODERATE INDIRECT- AND LOW-LIGHT PLANTS can live comfortably 8 feet (2.4 m) or more from a southern window, or close to a northern window. In the wild, these plants typically live in partial to full shade below the closed canopy of a forest.

Identifying Light Problems

TOO MUCH LIGHT

- Foliage becomes faded, washed out, or dull, or turns reddish pink (when it should be green)
- Leaves turn brown and crispy or develop patches

NOT ENOUGH LIGHT

- The space between leaves or buds lengthens
- Growth appears weak and leans toward a light source
- Variegated foliage becomes entirely green
- Leaves yellow and fall off
- Flowering plants fail to flower or produce just a few flowers

LIGHT METERS

You can use a light meter to measure the amount of light your plants receive. Typical light meters report light intensity as foot-candles. For reference: full sun equals about 5,000 foot-candles; bright indirect light 800 to 1,000 foot-candles; and anything below 800 foot-candles moderate indirect or low light.

Light Tips & Tricks

- Light intensity varies throughout the year, so move your plants accordingly. In summer, you may need to shift plants away from windows that receive direct light. In winter, move them as close to the window as possible, unless your windows are especially drafty. (Typical insulated windows are usually fine; be cautious if you can feel air moving through the frame.)

- Light is also heat. Eastern-facing windows receive morning light, which is cooler than the afternoon light of a western window. Choose eastern windows for delicate plants that need limited direct or morning light.

- Keep your windows clean. It makes a difference in the light your plants receive.

- If you must move a plant into different light conditions, keep in mind that modest decreases in light intensity are easier for a plant to handle than increases. A full-sun plant moved to bright indirect–light conditions will generally adapt, though you should expect some signs of stress, including leaf loss, reduced flowering, and less vigor. This type of change is best enacted for only a short period (perhaps during the winter months); ideally, you'd eventually return the plant to its preferred light condition. Low-light plants can't be moved to brighter light without risk of severe stress and decline. For more best practices when moving your plants, see page 29.

ARTIFICIAL LIGHT

To prolong the growth of tropical plants, use artificial lights to extend hours of "daylight" or provide more intense light in winter. Artificial lights also let you move plants freely around a room, regardless of the intensity of light they prefer.

When configuring your lighting system, the strength of the bulb and its proximity to the plant are important. Pay attention to the light's PPF (photosynthetic photon flux) or PPFD (photosynthetic photon flux density). These are measures of usable light; the higher the number, the more light energy a plant will receive. (Don't confuse these metrics with a bulb's wattage, which is how much energy it needs to produce light, rather than how much energy that light produces.) Generally, flowering plants need greater intensity, with a light source located 6 to 12 inches (15 to 30 cm) from the plant, while foliage-only plants require less intensity and a light placed 12 to 24 inches (30 to 61 cm) away.

WATERING

Watering is perhaps the most feared element of houseplant care, because it's where many plant parents either overindulge or fall prey to forgetfulness or inconsistency. We'll give individual guidance for each of the plants featured in this book, but watering should ultimately be tailored to your plant *and* your home.

Understanding Your Plant's Water Needs

While there's no perfect formula for when and how to water, answering the questions below can help you create the best routine for your plant.

WHAT ARE YOUR PLANT'S ORIGINS? Is it native to a desert, near-desert, temperate, subtropical, or tropical environment? Each of these habitats has a different rainfall pattern that your plant species has genetically adapted to over thousands of years.

IS YOUR PLANT ACTIVELY GROWING? If your plant is producing new leaves or is about to bloom, it needs an even supply of water—no skipped waterings or overwatering. If its growth is slowing down, it has finished blooming, or it is resting, then water is less imperative. Many plants prefer to be drier while they rest.

HOW MUCH LIGHT IS YOUR PLANT GETTING? More light means more photosynthesis, which in turn requires more water. Leafy plants in lower light will see slower moisture evaporation, so less water is better. Succulents are an exception; they're adapted to store water differently than other plants, so they can withstand heat and sun without frequent watering.

HOW BIG IS YOUR PLANT AND HOW MUCH SOIL IS IT GROWING IN? A small plant in a big pot of soil can easily drown; its roots are not developed enough to use all the water in the soil. Conversely, a big plant in little soil will require frequent watering.

WHAT KIND OF POT IS YOUR PLANT IN? Clay pots wick water from the soil, so they dry faster than nonporous plastic or glazed ceramic pots. (For more on pot choices, see page 14.)

WHAT KIND OF SOIL IS YOUR PLANT IN?
Chunkier soils made of bark or gravel drain
quickly and don't retain moisture long. Finer
potting soils (which often have a base of peat
moss) can take more time and water to wet but
retain moisture longer. Be cautious with these
finer soils; if they dry too much, they shrink and
become difficult to rehydrate. (For more on soil,
see page 16.)

WHAT IS THE TEMPERATURE AND HUMIDITY
SURROUNDING YOUR PLANT? Air can be a terrible
water thief—dry, hot air will steal moisture from
your plant and its soil. Increasing the humidity
around a plant (see page 26) will reduce water
loss from transpiration (the process by which
plants absorb, circulate, and release water) and
evaporation.

Your answers to the previous questions will
help you establish a watering program—but
remember that it may require adjustment over
time. Once again, observation is key. Set a
schedule to check on your plants, then use these
techniques to determine if they need water:

- If a plant is small enough to handle, feel its
  weight when it's wet, when it's damp, then
  when it's a bit dry. Once you understand the
  difference between these conditions, you'll have
  an easy way to judge moisture levels.
- Touch the soil surface and, if possible, put your
  finger into the soil up to a knuckle to learn what
  wet, damp, and dry soils feel like.
- Finally, look for signs that your plant is unhappy.
  Crispy brown leaf edges, limp leaves, and
  premature flower drop are signs of underwatering.
  Mushy leaves, browning leaf tips, yellowing
  leaves, mold, and rot are signs of too much water.

How to Water

The objective of watering is to saturate the soil—
not the plant—so situate the tip of the can's spout
under and away from foliage. Water gradually
until it drains from the bottom of the pot into a
saucer. Allow excess water to sit in the saucer for
thirty minutes, then drain. If the plant cannot be
moved, you can empty a full saucer with a turkey
baster.

Smaller, moisture-loving plants appreciate an
occasional immersion of their pot in a full saucer
or bowl of water, so that water can soak upward
through their soil. Allow to soak until the soil is
saturated, then remove the pot from the water and
drain before returning it to the original saucer.

Watering Tips & Tricks

- Plants are sensitive to the chemicals in tap
  water, so collect and use fresh rainwater as much
  as possible. If using tap, let it sit in an open
  container for twenty-four hours before watering
  to evaporate the chlorines and fluorides added
  to most municipal water sources.
- Let water reach room temperature before using.
  The extremes of hot and cold water can damage
  a plant.
- For plants that need even moisture at all times,
  consider investing in self-watering clay stakes or
  a self-watering pot.

FERTILIZER

Fertilizing houseplants can be confusing. Plants require different nutrients at different times in different quantities, and some nutrients leach out of the soil more quickly than others. But fertilizer is a necessity for healthy plants, as it provides the nutrients required to maintain growth. We'll give individual guidance for fertilizing each of the plants in this book, but here are the basics.

START WITH QUALITY POTTING SOIL. Potting soil is often nutrient enhanced or amended with slow-release fertilizers, so good soil can maintain a plant's health for four to six months without additional fertilizers. (The exact length of time will depend on how often you're watering and how hungry the plant is.) Let a freshly potted plant settle into its new soil and environment before starting a fertilizing program.

LOOK FOR SIGNS FROM YOUR PLANT. Your plant may be due for a meal if you see these signs: off-color appearance; production of skinny stems; flower production stopping before it should; internodes (the space between leaves or buds) that are long and weak or, conversely, stunted; leaves dropping; small and misshapen new leaves. In these cases, fertilize as recommended, but don't overdo it. (When it comes to fertilizer, more is not better.) If the leaves are the color they're supposed to be and you see new growth with short internodes in the right season (typically spring and/or summer), then your plant is getting the nutrition it needs. If you feed it during this time, do so lightly (at half the manufacturer's recommended rate for any given fertilizer) with at least two weeks or four to six waterings between feedings.

REDUCE DURING REST PERIODS. Many plants experience periods of rest, when most new growth stops because conditions are less than optimal (typically because the days are too short to support a plant's photosynthetic needs). Though the plant is still green, it's essentially hibernating. During this time, reduce fertilizing to once a month, if at all. Resting plants often need less water, which means less of the fertilizer ingredients will leach from the soil. This can cause a harmful accumulation of the chemical "salt" found in most fertilizers if applications aren't limited.

How to Choose Fertilizer

The phrase "up, down, and around" will help you remember fertilizer basics. Nitrogen, phosphorus, and potassium are macronutrients that every plant needs, and they affect three key growth areas: nitrogen fuels green leaves and stems (up); phosphorus promotes root growth (down); and potassium supports fruit and flower production (around).

There are both organic and chemical fertilizers on the market; either type will be labeled with a set of three numbers known as an NPK value. These numbers express the percentage by volume of nitrogen, phosphorus, and potassium respectively. If you're just getting started with houseplants or want a streamlined program, use a fertilizer with an even 10-10-10 NPK value. (Some might argue that this is a waste; plants don't need as much phosphorus or potassium when they're adding lots of foliage, and an injection of nitrogen may cause a flush of leaves instead of flowers when a plant is about to bloom. But for most home growers, providing a balanced formulation will offer houseplants the nutrition they need at all stages of their lives.)

As your growing skills advance, you can play with specific fertility programs based on the time and investment you want to make. For example, a high-nitrogen fertilizer is best for plants that will be only vegetative (all leaves, no flowers or fruit), while a formula low in nitrogen but high in potassium and phosphorus is best for plants approaching fruit or flower production.

Fertilizing Tips & Tricks

- For regular plant maintenance, our typical recommendation is a balanced liquid fertilizer, diluted in water.
- Generally speaking, most plants benefit from application of a slow-release pellet fertilizer when potting.
- Consider the fact that the plant's growth will be impacted by the amount of feeding you do; when it comes to larger trees we typically recommend fertilizing sparingly so these plants don't outgrow your space too quickly.
- The more often a plant is watered, the more fertilizer it can tolerate (and may need, because of leaching). Almost all chemical fertilizers deliver nutrients in the form of chemical salts. When plants are infrequently watered, these salts can accumulate in the soil and cause root damage. Larger trees, succulents, and cacti are particularly susceptible to this, and thus should be fertilized sparingly.

TEMPERATURE

Houseplants' temperature preferences are often misunderstood. It's true that cold is the kiss of death for most tropical and subtropical species, but 99 percent of houseplants don't like it *hot*. The sweet spot for temperature in your home is 60 to 75°F (15 to 24°C). Above that, a plant's metabolic activity will slow or stop altogether, which eventually leads to death. Some plants' needs are even more specific; we've noted any unusual temperature requirements for the plants profiled in the pages that follow.

Many plants experience periods of rest (see opposite); during this time, they prefer temperatures on the lower end of the range above. However, dramatic changes of 20°F (12°C) up or down can shock and kill a plant instantly, so avoid drafts and move houseplants away from drafty windows or gusty doorways in wintertime.

AIR MOVEMENT

A house gives your plants the luxury of protection, but with walls come some losses—including a lack of wind and fresh air. Exposure to gentle wind is essential to the health of most plants; it replaces stale and tired air with fresh air, dries leaves if they are too wet, strengthens stems as they resist its pressure, cools the plant, and cleans it, too. If possible, introduce air movement around your plants with a fan or cross ventilation—but avoid cold drafts, hot blowing air, and strong gusts.

HUMIDITY

Watering is the first thing that comes to mind when talking about houseplants and moisture, but humidity is equally critical. Jungle air hovers around 70 to 90 percent humidity, air on a comfortable day in a temperate climate falls between 40 and 60 percent, and desert air ranges from 10 to 30 percent. A warm winter home can approach desertlike levels of humidity because the heated air creates a water vacuum, sucking up any available moisture—and your plants are often the source of that moisture, so they'll feel particularly parched.

While desert plants are well adapted to low humidity and shouldn't need additional moisture in the air, tropical, subtropical, and temperate plants are easily stressed by dry conditions. If your houseplants require extra humidity, there are a few methods to consider.

MISTING: To increase local humidity around your plants, spritz with a mister or spray bottle. Spray as early in the day as possible, with a fine mist: large water beads can act as a magnifying glass and burn foliage in full sun, or dry too slowly (leaves that remain wet overnight can foster diseases). Tepid tap water or ambient-temperature rainwater is best for misting. Applying water directly on the leaves discourages spider mites (see page 33), beneficially lowers the plant's temperature, and deters dust. Do not mist buds or flowers; this can fade flowers prematurely, abort buds, or cause a fungal condition called botrytis (see page 32). Plants with velvety or hairy leaves can't tolerate wet foliage; instead, use one of the next two methods.

HUMIDITY TRAY: If misting is too time-consuming or not appropriate for your plants, try a humidity tray (shown opposite). This method is also great for very dry spaces, because it creates a humid microclimate around your plants. Fill a tray with pebbles or place a support block at its center, then add water to fill the tray. Place your plant on top, without submerging its pot. Top off water daily.

DOUBLE POTTING: If humidity trays make your space feel cluttered, double potting is a good alternative. Choose a waterproof container or cachepot that's larger than the pot your houseplant is in, fill it with peat moss, then place your potted houseplant inside. Keep the peat moss moist (do not pour water onto the houseplant directly). This method also has enormous thermal-insulating benefits if your houseplant happens to be near a hot or cold window.

Humidity Tips & Tricks

- Try grouping plants together to naturally create a microclimate with higher humidity.
- Invest in a humidifier (or two) to place near your most humidity-loving plants.
- Place tropical plants (which are used to generous rainfall) temporarily in your shower and create an at-home "rainstorm." This waters the plants and gives them a humidity bath while also cleaning their leaves and mitigating certain pest problems. Before placing your plants in a shower, be sure the water temperature is just warm enough (not cold or hot) and the pressure is soft.
- If a plant requires high humidity, consider placing it in a well-lit bathroom; your daily showers will provide ambient humidity.
- To increase overall ambient humidity in a larger area of your home, boil a pot of water on your stovetop. This is especially helpful on successive cold, dry winter days.

PRUNING

Whether you prune your plants to shape them is a matter of preference; some people like wild, unpruned silhouettes, while others prefer tidier forms. You will need to prune to remove dead, broken, or diseased parts of your plant—or to "deadhead," which entails pinching or cutting off dead flowers to promote more flowering.

Pruning Tips & Tricks

• Use sharp, disinfected pruners.
• Always make your cuts just above a node (see page 35) when pruning plants with branches, or cut to the ground when a plant grows as a group of individual stems that emerge from the soil. For tubers (such as alocasia, page 206) cut spent leaves close to the base of the petiole.
• To encourage branching for a fuller silhouette, you can use your thumb and forefinger to pinch off tender new growth at the end of a stem.

LEAF CARE

Houseplants will collect dust if not regularly misted or given occasional showers (see page 26). Because plants breathe through their leaves, a layer of dust can suffocate them. Dust also obstructs light, causing plants to decline. Smaller plants can be rinsed monthly in the kitchen sink, while larger plants will enjoy a light shower. Remember to use only tepid water and a gentle stream from the faucet or showerhead. Dust larger, immobile plants with a cloth every week or two, then wipe their leaves with tepid tap water and a sponge every few months. When cleaning leaves, give them as much support as possible to prevent tearing. We don't recommend using plant polishes; they contain waxes and oils that clog the stomas (microscopic pores that allow a plant to expel gas and water vapor, which is essential to the photosynthesis process). In essence, they limit the plant's ability to breathe. We also prefer a clean, natural look rather than the unnatural high shine of a polished plant.

MOVING YOUR PLANTS

Plants are relatively stationary beings—and they would prefer to stay that way. They struggle with flux and extremes: intense heat or cold, drastic changes in temperature, drafts, cold or hot water, sudden repositioning, or changes in light. That said, change is good when it improves a plant's growing situation (for example, moving it outdoors into fresh air and better-quality light during the summer). The best rule of thumb is to introduce new conditions gradually and avoid rapid change if a plant is about to flower. And keep close tabs on your plants throughout the process— they'll show you what they need, if you're paying attention.

Tips & Tricks for Moving Your Plants

- Avoid moving a plant more than once every few months. Acclimating takes energy, so a plant may lose its vigor if forced to adapt repeatedly.
- If you have a plant that's lopsided because it's leaning toward a light source, methodically turning the plant will encourage more even growth. Rotate the plant one quarter turn each time you water, except when buds or flowers develop; any movement during that time can abort blooms prematurely.

Transitioning Houseplants Outdoors

A temporary relocation outdoors during spring and summer can be beneficial for many houseplants. Citrus trees, palms, succulents, alocasias, and larger tropicals all appreciate a warm growing season after a winter indoors; an outdoor field trip will bolster their strength before they head back inside for fall. If you have a plant

suffering from pest issues, the additional airflow and ventilation found outside helps alleviate many concerns. Hardier aroids like monsteras and philodendrons can do well in dappled outdoor light, too. More tender specimens, such as ferns and calatheas, should not be moved outdoors.

If your plants are well suited for a change of scenery, this big transition must happen in stages; houseplants need a slow introduction to the more intense outdoor sun. Once overnight temperatures regularly stay above 60°F (15°C), move plants to a sheltered, shady outdoor location. (A covered porch against your house is ideal.) Every few days, move plants into more intense light until they reach their final location— this process can take up to two weeks.

When choosing your plants' ultimate outdoor location, keep their light requirements in mind. Full-shade plants need to stay in full shade, full-sun plants can move to full outdoor sun, and bright indirect–light plants can enjoy early-morning sun but need shade or protection for most of the day. In addition, select a place that's sheltered from the wind for plants whose leaves can be damaged by blustery conditions, such as palms. At summer's end, return your plants indoors when nighttime temperatures approach 50°F (10°C). Expect some leaf loss; lower light intensity means less photosynthesis, so plants can't support as much foliage.

REPOTTING

While some vigorous tropical houseplants love a yearly "up potting" (being transferred to a slightly larger pot), most houseplants prefer less-frequent moves. Repotting is, after all, a traumatic root disturbance—not all plants appreciate or recover quickly from it—so it's best to allow most plants to become pot-bound before repotting.

How can you tell if a plant is pot-bound? A pot-bound plant typically fills its entire pot. You may notice that its color seems off, that it shows reduced vigor in spite of fertilizer applications, or that it needs especially frequent watering (a signal that there's too little soil to hold water). You may also spot roots poking from the pot's drainage hole.

Slow-growing plants don't react well to frequent disturbances from repotting. In addition, some flowering plants, like the African violet (page 70) and giant white bird-of-paradise (page 209), need to be slightly pot-bound before they produce flowers, because they require a stressor to initiate reproduction. We've noted any unusual potting requirements like these for the plants profiled in the pages that follow. But most should be repotted when you spot signs that they're pot-bound.

If repotting is necessary, try to complete the process just before or as new growth begins. This is typically in spring, but the timing may vary based on the plant's seasonal rhythm.

How to Repot

1. At least an hour before repotting, water your plant well and let it drain.
2. To remove a plant from its old container, start by cutting back any protruding roots from the drainage hole. If the plant is in a plastic pot, push on the sides of the pot to loosen the root-ball. If the plant is in an inflexible pot, lightly tap the sides of the pot against the palm of your hand. Do not pull on the plant to lift it; instead, place your hand on the soil surface around the stem and invert the pot. If the plant will not dislodge, carefully run a knife around the inner edge of the pot and try again.
3. Once the plant has been removed, inspect the roots. If they are loosely wrapped, gently break up the root-ball with your fingers (as shown opposite). If they are more tightly wrapped, use a knife or pruners to very lightly score the lower half of the root-ball. Cuts should be no more than ¼ to ½ inch (6 mm to 1.3 cm) deep. Depending on the size of the root ball, six to twelve scores should be sufficient.
4. When positioning your plant in a new pot, leave enough space at the top to hold some water and prevent spillage. Many pots have a molded lip that's a great guide to how high you should set the upper surface of your plant. A medium-size tabletop planter should have at least a 2-inch (5 cm) gap between the soil surface and the top of the pot.
5. Put just enough soil in the bottom of the pot to set your plant into place at the correct height, then backfill once the plant is positioned. Lightly press down and around the edges of the soil to fill any air pockets. (No need to press hard.)
6. Water and let drain for a few minutes, then water and let drain again. It may take a few waterings in quick succession to wet new potting mix.

PESTS & DISEASES

The best way to avoid pests and diseases is to select a clean, healthy plant and give it proper care in a clean environment. Two other general prevention tips: First, isolate new plants coming into your home until you're confident that they're healthy. Second, carefully examine your plants every time you water them. Look under leaves, in between branches, and along stems for signs of pests, fungi, or disease. Early detection makes remediation much easier. All that said, sometimes pests and diseases happen in spite of every caution, so here is an overview of general houseplant ailments and their remedies.

APHIDS: These sucking insects come in many colors; you may spot solid green, peach, orange, or black bodies. Aphids feed on tender new growth and reproduce at a phenomenal rate (females are born pregnant!). To combat them, spray them off with water or smush them between your fingers. Note: Aphids produce a secretion called honeydew—more on this at right.

BOTRYTIS: This gray mold thrives in damp, cool environments. It's most often found growing on fruit and flowers that remain wet overnight. To prevent it, water in the morning to give the plant ample time to dry. Do not get fruit or flowers wet. If infection occurs, prune away infected parts of the plant.

FUNGUS GNATS: These tiny black flies are generally harmless but are unsightly and annoying. They lay eggs on damp soil surfaces, and their larvae (maggots) feed primarily on organic matter in the soil, but they can damage plant roots. Gnats are best avoided by allowing soil surfaces to dry between waterings.

HONEYDEW: This is the sticky excrement of insects including aphids, mealybugs, scale, and whiteflies. Honeydew is the primary source of sooty mold. Ants will "farm" honeydew-producing aphids, mealybugs, and scale to collect this secretion; if you see ants, there is likely another pest on the plant.

MEALYBUGS: Round, soft-bodied insects covered in white, waxy "fluff," mealybugs thrive in warm, moist environments and tend to cluster along stems, under leaves, and along leaf veins. They are easily wiped away with a damp cloth or cotton swab, but total eradication is difficult once a plant is heavily infested. Note: Mealybugs produce honeydew.

OEDEMA (EDEMA): This hard, lumpy growth on the underside of the leaf is caused by too much water and not enough light. An affected plant cannot transpire enough water through its leaves, so the excess water ruptures cells. To remedy, reduce watering, increase air circulation, and increase light intensity. Remove damaged foliage.

ROT: Rot occurs when healthy plant tissue becomes soft, brown, and mushy. It can manifest anywhere on a plant and is caused by a multitude of pathogens. In general, wet conditions, poor ventilation, and too high or too low temperatures precede the onset of disease. Early detection and removal of rotting tissue can sometimes save a plant, but in most cases, without extreme chemical intervention, the plant and soil must be discarded and the vessel disinfected. Proper plant care is key to prevention.

SCALE: These round, soft-bodied insects tend to cluster along stems, under leaves, and along leaf veins. They cover themselves with waxy brown shells as adults, rendering them immobile—and thus easily wiped away with a damp cloth or cotton swab; total eradication is difficult, however, because immature scale are mobile and hard to see until they develop their waxy coating. Note: Scale produce honeydew.

SOOTY MOLD: An unsightly black fungus that grows on honeydew, sooty mold prevents light from reaching plants' leaves. To remedy, clean affected leaves with a damp cloth and manage any possible pest infestations that cause honeydew, such as aphids, mealybugs, scale, and whiteflies.

SPIDER MITES: These almost microscopic pests feed on the underside of the leaf, causing stippling or a silver to bronze sheen on foliage. Their tiny black excrement, called frass, is more visible than they are; so are their webs. If you see webbing, however, your mite population has exploded. They thrive in dry conditions, so regular misting or rinsing off foliage in the sink or shower helps control their populations.

WHITEFLIES: These tiny white insects cluster under leaves. A gentle shake will expose populations, which will fly off only to return to the host plant or infest new plants. Whiteflies are pernicious and difficult to control without chemical intervention. Place sticky whitefly traps around vulnerable plants if you suspect an infestation. Note: Whiteflies produce honeydew.

PESTS & DISEASES

Aphids

Botrytis

Fungus Gnats

Honeydew

Mealybugs

Oedema (Edema)

Rot

Scale

Sooty Mold

Spider Mites

Whiteflies

PROPAGATION

What's better than having one houseplant? Having two houseplants. Or maybe three. How about a dozen or more to share with friends?! Many houseplants can be multiplied at home using the propagation methods outlined in the following pages. Propagation is great for sharing the houseplant love, and it can also extend your relationship with a specimen plant that has aged, lost its vigor, or developed a less-attractive shape—with propagation, you can grow a new plant to replace the one that's in decline.

At-home propagation can be achieved in conjunction with some plants' natural reproduction methods (offsets and plantlets). Propagation via cuttings, whether in water or soil, is one of the most common methods for multiplying your houseplants—if you're new to propagation, simply placing a cutting in water and waiting for it to root is the easiest way to begin. Finally, seed sowing, though not the most common form of houseplant propagation, is the only option for some rare plants

that can't be procured from a grower. The profiles that follow will note which method to use if the plant can successfully be propagated at home.

Divisions, Offsets & Plantlets

Divisions, offsets, and plantlets are, in essence, a houseplant's attempts to propagate itself. Because the plant does a lot of the work, propagation with the methods described below can be a great option for home growers. When you spot an opportunity for this type of propagation, be patient; wait until the new stems, offsets, or plantlets are large and sturdy enough to be handled before separating them from the parent plant.

DIVISION is a technique used for clumping plants like maranta (page 90), which develop expanding root systems that send up new stems or rosettes from the base of the plant. These new plants can be separated from the mother by dividing the root system and pulling the plants apart, then repotting them separately. (You may need a knife to cut away the plants.)

OFFSETS are juvenile plants that develop at the base of a mother plant's stem and may not have roots of their own. Cut these away from the mother plant as close to the stem as possible and pot like a stem cutting (see page 36).

PLANTLETS, OR "PUPS," are juvenile plants with roots that develop at the end of a mother plant's flower stems or along its leaf edges (see an example on page 161). These can be carefully harvested and inserted at least ½ inch (1.3 cm) into a light potting mix. Keep moist while roots form.

Plant Anatomy 101

When propagating a plant via cuttings, you'll need to first harvest part of the plant: a stem; a whole leaf plus as much petiole (stalk or stem) as possible; or part of a leaf, which is suited for stemless plants like sansevieria (page 120). Cuttings taken from the tip of a branch are called top cuttings and typically include an apical bud. Because the plant is already focusing energy on growth here, it will continue to grow vertically. An internode cutting, by contrast, can result in lateral growth.

Once you've collected your cuttings, a stem or whole leaf cutting with petiole can be propagated in water; any type of cutting can be propagated in soil. (Note: Succulent leaves do not have petioles, thus they have their own propagation method—see page 36.)

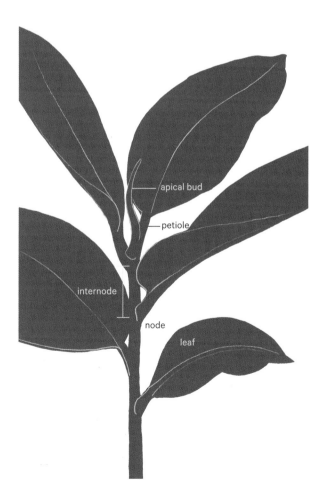

Propagating Cuttings in Water

1. *For a stem cutting*, cut a 3- to 6-inch (8 to 15 cm) length of nonflowering stem, just under a node, and remove any leaves from the lower half of the cutting. *For a whole leaf cutting*, remove a healthy leaf with its petiole from the stem.
2. Fill a clean, glass vessel with room-temperature distilled water.
3. *For a stem cutting*, insert the stem into the water up to at least a node. You may submerge more of the stem, but do not submerge any leaves. *For a whole leaf cutting*, submerge the entire petiole.
4. Place in bright indirect light and be patient. Top off with tepid water as needed. If the water becomes cloudy, empty and disinfect the vessel and refill with fresh water. Over the course of a few weeks, new roots will emerge from the nodes or the cut end of the petiole. When the roots are at least a few inches (5 to 8 cm) long (as shown opposite), pot following the instructions on page 37, or let the plant continue to grow in water.

A. Stem cutting   B. Whole leaf cutting   C. Partial leaf cutting
D. Succulent leaf cutting

Propagating Cuttings in Soil

STEM CUTTING

1. Cut a 3- to 6-inch (8 to 15 cm) length of nonflowering stem, just under a leaf or stem node.
2. Remove any leaves from the lower half of the cutting.
3. Dip the cut end into rooting hormone (see opposite), following the manufacturer's instructions, and insert at least ½ inch (1.3 cm) into a light potting mix, covering at least one node. Press the soil around the stem and water gently. Keep moist while roots form.

WHOLE LEAF CUTTING

1. Remove a healthy leaf with its petiole from the stem and dip the cut end into rooting hormone, following the manufacturer's instructions.
2. Insert at least ½ inch (1.3 cm) into a light potting mix. Stalked leaves, like those of an African violet, can be inserted almost to the leaf's bottom edge. Keep moist while roots form.

PARTIAL LEAF CUTTING

1. Remove a healthy leaf from the stem, then cut the leaf into pieces, being sure to capture a vein and/or edge. For linear leaves like sansevieria, a 2- to 3-inch (5 to 8 cm) crosscut is sufficient; rounded leaves can be cut into 2-inch (5 cm) pie-shaped wedges.
2. Dip the cut end into rooting hormone, following the manufacturer's instructions. Insert the cut section at least ½ inch (1.3 cm) into a light potting mix, and keep moist while roots form.

SUCCULENT LEAF CUTTING

1. Remove a healthy leaf from a stem.
2. Let dry for a few days to naturally seal the cut end before inserting at least 1½ inches (1.3 cm) into initially moist, very-well-draining potting soil. Be sensitive about watering succulent cuttings, as they will rot easily; misting is best if the soil appears dusty or too dry.

- All cuttings should be made with a sharp knife or razor blade and taken from the healthiest parts of actively growing plants.
- Cut ends are fragile, and if dusted with rooting hormone (see below), should not be shoved directly into even a light potting or germination mix. Using a pencil tip or dibber, predrill a small hole into the soil surface.
- Once inserted into potting mix, most cuttings need even soil moisture and regular misting to remain hydrated while roots form.
- Using a humidity bag is advisable: place the pot or tray of cuttings in a plastic bag, creating a "tent" to help maintain ambient moisture and soil moisture.
- Keep cuttings under bright light, but out of direct sun.
- Be patient! Don't tug on plants to see if they have rooted—you could break the fragile new roots as they're forming. It's best to avoid touching a cutting at all until you see new growth at either the tips or base. Only then should you very carefully lift and repot (see right). When lifting, don't pull on the new plant; loosen the soil around it and scoop up as much soil with the plant as possible. (If the plant is in a cell tray, pop out the whole cell by pushing up from the bottom.)

ROOTING HORMONE

Rooting hormone is a powder or liquid product available at most garden centers. It's made of plant auxins, which are chemical signals that program plants' cells; in this case, they tell the plant to make root cells instead of cells for stems or leaves. Rooting hormone increases the likelihood of root development from a cutting but doesn't guarantee it. As with all chemical products, handle with care.

Seed Sowing

Seeds are dormant plants waiting for their ideal growing conditions before they germinate and spring to life. Every seed has a particular formula for breaking dormancy; that may be scratching its seed coat (scarification) or experiencing a specific period of damp coldness followed by warmth (stratification), but some basics apply to most seed sowing at home: Start with a seed germinating mix, and use the smallest available container to start your seeds—multicelled seed-starting trays are the best option for beginners. Once sown, seeds need light, warmth, and consistent moisture to germinate. Beyond that, specifics will vary by plant. When it comes to this propagation method, a little research goes a long way.

Repotting Propagated Plants

Newly propagated plants should be moved to progressively larger pots in stages as they mature. Start with a vessel only a little larger than the volume of the soil your plant occupied during propagation. If the plant was propagated in water, the pot and soil should be no more than three times the volume of the root mass. When the roots of the plant fill this container, it can be moved to a slightly larger pot. Continue gradually repotting in larger vessels until you reach a size that's suitable for the mature plant.

ONE

TRENDSETTERS

AROID MANIA

I N THE EARLY SEVENTEENTH CENTURY, A TULIP OBSESSION swept the Netherlands. Investors spent astronomical sums on individual bulbs, snatching up rare mutations in a volatile speculative market—a period now known as "tulipomania." The plant world is experiencing another such moment right now: welcome to aroid mania.

"Aroid" is the common name for a member of the Araceae family, which includes überpopular houseplants like monstera, anthurium, and philodendron. Many of these tropical trendsetters were ubiquitous in the 1960s and '70s; now they're back in a big way, delighting avid collectors and casual green thumbs alike. If you need a single houseplant with major visual impact, an aroid is the perfect choice.

What makes aroids so compelling? Two words: fantastic foliage. Each species possesses leaves of exceptional shape, color, and texture. Within the family, you'll find sharply dissected edges, lacy fenestrations, prominent veins, and plush velvety surfaces, all in a dazzling range of hues. In addition, many aroids undergo a pronounced transformation as they reach maturity, their leaves morphing to take on the appearance of an entirely different plant.

Though their foliage takes center stage, there's lots more to love about aroids. They're diverse in scale, available as lofty tree forms, petite tabletop specimens, and wandering vines. And they combine a high-impact appearance with unfussy care requirements. Simply keep these warmth-loving tropicals away from cold, drafty spaces; give their leaves an occasional cleaning; and watch them grow.

The meteoric rise of aroids began with the now-iconic *Monstera deliciosa* and has since ballooned into a collector's craze. Demand for uncommon varieties and variegations far outpaces supply from growers, who are just beginning to invest heavily in aroid cultivation. That means you might discover tiny specimens of hard-to-find plants selling for hundreds of dollars. But don't despair: our guide also includes more-accessible options.

PHILODENDRON

WHEN THEY HEAR "PHILODENDRON," many people think of the ever-popular pothos (page 114), but this verdant group of plants from the tropical Americas and West Indies is far more diverse. After a recent scientific split with terrestrial and tree-shaped *Thaumatophyllum* (page 47), genus *Philodendron* contains primarily vining plants. It's a fitting distinction; "philodendron" roughly translates to "tree-loving," a name no doubt inspired by these plants' tendency to climb the nearest trunk.

Thanks to philodendrons' recent rise in popularity, more varieties with interesting variegations and colors are becoming available all the time, as growers are putting them into tissue culture (more on this on page 62) and propagating older specimens that have been sitting in collections but haven't been sold commercially. Learn about a few of our favorites (including *Philodendron* 'Jose Buono', pictured at left), on pages 44–45.

Philodendrons offer a wide range of leaf shapes, from tiny ovals to gigantic elongated hearts. Like vining aroids, many philodendrons are sold with immature leaf forms that benefit from the addition of an organic support structure like a moss pole—see the vining aroids profile on page 54 for more.

Lush and lovely but less overtly tropical than many aroids, philodendrons range in size from modest tabletop plants to large specimens that can anchor a room. They're adaptable to indirect light and unfussy as long as their watering and humidity needs are met, giving the instant gratification of rambling greenery without a demanding care routine.

LIGHT • Moderate to bright indirect light; avoid direct sun.

WATER • Keep the soil consistently moist; watering once per week is usually sufficient.

HUMIDITY • Benefits from humidity.

SOIL • Well-draining potting mix amended with organic matter and orchid bark or other aggregates for added drainage, nutrition, and structure.

FERTILIZER • In the growing season (spring to fall), feed with a balanced or high-nitrogen liquid fertilizer once a month at half the manufacturer's recommended rate. When plant growth slows in winter, stop fertilizing.

PESTS & DISEASE • Watch for speckling on the leaves, which can be a sign of mite damage.

SHOPPING • Choose philodendrons with upright, fairly rigid stems and leaves. Soft, droopy foliage indicates an unhealthy plant. Start with a philodendron slightly smaller than the size you ultimately want—they're vigorous growers.

POTTING • Mature plants benefit from the addition of a structure with an organic surface, like a moss pole.

PROPAGATION • Can be propagated with stem cuttings in soil or water.

PHILODENDRON

Philodendron
'Birkin'

A cross between *Philodendron* 'Congo' and *P.* 'Imperial Green', this compact new cultivar has petite, oval leaves with exceedingly fine white-on-green variegation that follows along the veins. Be careful when choosing a specimen because 'Birkin' can revert, meaning it can lose its variegated appearance. Opt for one with consistent coloration and avoid those with emerging leaves that are solid green or red—a sign that the plant is reverting.

Philodendron
'Jose Buono'

Large, irregular oval leaves with subtly wavy edges are the defining feature of this fun and accessible philodendron. 'Jose Buono' gains additional character from inconsistent variegations, which range from tiny speckles to half-and-half divisions of white and green. For display, pair it with an upright urn that emphasizes its graceful shape, and provide support to keep its huge leaves from toppling over.

Philodendron erubescens
'Pink Princess'

Once ubiquitous but more recently available solely from collectors, this highly sought-after pink philodendron is finally reentering the houseplant market at large. Its spade-shaped leaves feature irregular variegations of vivid pink and moody deep green, ranging in pattern from speckles to crisply divided halves. New foliage often emerges red and transitions to pink over time, adding further color interest.

Philodendron hastatum
Silver sword

This modestly sized vining philodendron will be similar in scale to a pothos as a young plant. Though smaller than many of its relatives, it stands out thanks to the glaucous, iridescent sheen of its leaves. This soft, silvery hue is especially good for adding contrast in collections that feature brighter green specimens.

THAUMATOPHYLLUM

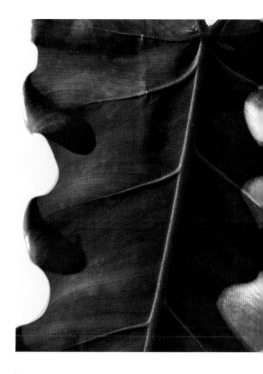

IF YOU'RE A LONGTIME PLANT LOVER, you may recognize the specimen pictured here as a philodendron—and until recently, you would have been right. The aroid family underwent a scientific shake-up in 2018, when botanists used DNA testing to determine that some philodendrons actually belong to an existing but less-familiar genus: *Thaumatophyllum*. Essentially, this discovery divided philodendrons by growth habit. Those now classified as thaumatophyllum are terrestrial understory dwellers with a trunk-like structure, while true philodendrons are vines. This means that plants you might think of as "tree philodendrons" are likely to be thaumatophyllums.

The change from philodendron to thaumatophyllum is so new that it hasn't fully taken hold among growers, so you may find these plants still labeled as philodendrons at your local nursery (for example, the specimen pictured on page 22 is frequently found as *Philodendron goeldii*). Regardless of name, thaumatophyllums possess the same showy character that we've always loved about tree philodendrons. Native to South American jungles, their broad leaves evoke the abundance of their tropical habitat. Mature specimens have a wide silhouette formed by large leaves that sprout from a central trunk. The lower leaves fall away as the plant grows, revealing a trunk that develops wild, unexpected texture over time.

This treelike silhouette is quite impactful at maturity, making larger specimens well suited for display as floor plants. For added interest, the open space at the base of the trunk easily accommodates an underplanting; here we've paired *Thaumatophyllum stenolobum* with *Pilea glauca* 'Aquamarine'. If you have a smaller plant, elevate it to eye level using a tall container or stand, so its lush greenery and splendid form can be admired.

LIGHT • Moderate to bright indirect light; avoid direct sun.

WATER • Water in moderation and keep the soil consistently moist. These plants struggle in waterlogged soil or if allowed to dry out completely. Crisp brown leaf edges are a sign of underwatering, while allover brown and yellow spots indicate overwatering.

HUMIDITY • Thrives in humidity.

SOIL • Well-draining potting mix amended with organic matter and orchid bark or other aggregates for added drainage, nutrition, and structure.

FERTILIZER • In the growing season (spring to fall), feed with a balanced or high-nitrogen liquid fertilizer once a month at half the manufacturer's recommended rate. When plant growth slows in winter, stop fertilizing.

SHOPPING • Buy these moderate growers to fit the space you have in mind. Immature plants are usually sold in 6- to 10-inch (15 to 25 cm) pots and will already be the size of a tabletop houseplant. If you want the distinctive look of the trunk, purchase a more mature specimen.

ANTHURIUM

LIGHT • Moderate to bright indirect light.

WATER • Water when the top 2 inches (5 cm) of soil become dry. Brown leaf tips indicate a lack of moisture. Don't overwater; though they like moisture, anthurium plants can rot.

HUMIDITY • Benefits from humidity.

SOIL • Well-draining potting mix amended with organic matter and orchid bark or other aggregates for added drainage, nutrition, and structure.

FERTILIZER • In the growing season (spring to fall), feed with a balanced liquid or high-nitrogen fertilizer once a month at half the manufacturer's recommended rate. When plant growth slows in winter, stop fertilizing.

SHOPPING • Because these plants are so collectible, prices for mature specimens can be high; you are likely to see smaller sizes at your local plant shop.

FLOWERING ANTHURIUMS have long been a popular choice of designers who need an unfussy, slow-growing plant with a pop of color; you've likely seen anthuriums' vivid, waxy blooms gracing plantings in the lobby of your local mall or office building. Though well deserved, the *Anthurium* genus's reputation for reliable blooms conceals its exciting diversity when it comes to foliage-forward varieties. It's these impressive leaves that make anthuriums darlings among the newly aroid-obsessed.

In this under-the-radar group, you'll find textured surfaces that range from plush and velvety to rigid and leathery, splashed with a painter's palette of rich blacks, saturated greens, and dramatic variegations. (One of our favorite variegated varieties, 'Thai Ruby', is pictured at left; see our specimen guide on the following pages for more.) Anthurium foliage is intriguingly architectural, replete with deep dissections, upright ruffles, graceful lances, and even charming hearts. When you choose a foliage-forward specimen (unlike varieties with colorful, waxy blooms), you can really appreciate its tall, spindly inflorescences, as seen in the image opposite. No matter their shape, the leaves grow outward from a central point, often perched atop a crown-like structure of exposed roots, creating an elegant silhouette.

Thanks to their ample color and textural interest, anthuriums are best displayed as stand-alone specimens—a role that suits their adaptability to challenging conditions. Native to tropical forest floors in the Western Hemisphere, these understory dwellers are very tolerant of indirect light, and thus can thrive deeper in a room with ambient light. They're slower to outgrow their spaces, so you can enjoy their vibrant presence for a long time and—thanks to their adaptability—in nearly any location.

ANTHURIUM

Anthurium sect. *Pachyneurium*
'Big Red Bird'

As its name suggests, this is among the largest and most colorful cultivars, with character that increases as it matures. It produces lance-shaped leaves with a crinkly, reptilian texture that turn from green to red in cooler temperatures. 'Big Red Bird' can be dense in habit, but it develops an airy shape with pronounced roots in lower-light situations. Tolerating limited humidity, it can be a good choice for adding a lush look in dry spaces.

Anthurium crystallinum
'Silver'

We love this plant for its velvety, heart-shaped, and deeply veined leaves, which grow in a cluster that flares upward and out. Its color is equally outstanding, ranging from dark green to black, with an iridescent sheen at maturity. To see the vaselike shape of this cultivar, turn to page 21.

Anthurium pedatoradiatum
'Fingers'

This cheerful cultivar is named for its hand-shaped leaves, which develop an increasing number of deeply dissected "digits" as they grow. Pronounced veins cover each leaf, trailing across the umbrella-shaped center and down the dangling fingers. Show off this finely textured variety in an urn or elevated planter.

Anthurium
'Thai Ruby'

This broad-leaved variety is especially showy, splashed with irregular patterns of white, pink, and green. While most variegated plants have clear delineations between colors, 'Thai Ruby' offers a painterly, layered look.
Note: While you might not see this particular tricolored specimen often, due to the frequency of open pollination in anthurium you can sometimes find quirky variegated forms that aren't necessarily a specific cultivar.

Monstera deliciosa

MONSTERA

OF ALL THE AROIDS IN THIS CHAPTER, none is more popular than *Monstera deliciosa*. Why? Quite simply, it's all about the leaves. They're big and bold, with heart-shaped surfaces lacquered in glossy green. And they're constantly evolving: As a monstera begins to mature, its leaf edges develop deep serrations, splitting to create its distinctive silhouette. Later in maturity, the leaves' once-solid interiors will develop holes called fenestrations.

M. deliciosa grows as a vine on trees in its native Mexico, so it prefers life as a climber. Your plant will benefit from the structure of a moss pole or a stake (attach with garden twine); while monstera stems are sturdy, they need support as the weighty leaves mature. Training the plant on a pole also produces a tidier shape, because the stems sprawl without support.

The classic green monstera (pictured at right) has captivated countless plant lovers—but if you want something more surprising, consider a variegated monstera, whose multicolored leaves add further interest to this striking species. *M. deliciosa* 'Albo Variegata' offers rare true white variegation; a genetic mutation creates its blocky patterns, including half-green/half-white and even fully white leaves. Another sought-after variety is *M. deliciosa* 'Thai Constellation' (pictured opposite and on pages 58–59), splashed with creamy yellow-white variegations in a starry pattern that inspires its celestial name.

Houseplant hunters are clamoring for these new faces, making them exceptionally hot commodities—and they're grown in a unique way. Because it's a genetic mutation, variegation isn't stable in plants grown from seed, so propagation is the only way to replicate prized patterns. Though you may find variegated specimens in a specialty plant shop, many collectors propagate their own from cuttings purchased online, which can be more affordable. (See page 35 for tips on finding reputable sources.) Monsteras grow quickly and can easily be propagated via cuttings, making them a good entry point into this technique. Once you've found a cutting you love, turn to page 34 for our propagation guide.

LIGHT • Bright indirect light.

WATER • Water when the top 2 inches (5 cm) of soil become dry.

HUMIDITY • Humidity is key, especially for variegated plants.

SOIL • Well-draining potting mix amended with organic matter and orchid bark or other aggregates for added drainage, nutrition, and structure.

FERTILIZER • In the growing season (spring to fall), feed with a balanced or high-nitrogen liquid fertilizer once a month at half the manufacturer's recommended rate. When plant growth slows in winter, stop fertilizing.

PESTS & DISEASE • Monsteras are susceptible to scale.

SHOPPING • Monsteras don't develop fenestrations until maturity; buy a more established plant to get the iconic leaf shape right away.

POTTING • Check your plant regularly for signs that it's becoming pot-bound and repot as needed.

PRUNING • Pruning can help regulate growth and shape. It's best done in early spring before the growing season begins. (This is also a good time to take cuttings for propagation.)

PROPAGATION • Can be propagated with stem cuttings in soil or water.

VINING AROIDS

ALONGSIDE ICONIC PLANTS like monsteras and philodendrons, the aroid family contains a wealth of approachable vining varieties. These low-maintenance plants have a particularly impressive presence, combining lofty habits with adaptable foliage: depending on how they're planted, vining aroids can either trail or climb. If allowed to trail without a support structure, the plant will continue to produce its immature leaf form (as seen in the *Rhaphidophora decursiva* 'Dragon Tail' pictured at left); try elevating a trailing plant in an urn or a hanging basket to make the most of its drapey silhouette. If given the option to climb, the foliage will eventually take on its mature form while creating a display with lots of linear vertical interest.

Note: This shift from immature to mature foliage is triggered by root development. Trailing plants get their nutrients from a single group of roots, while climbers grow roots along the length of the vine, providing additional water and nutrients to reach maturity. (In the wild, aroids are epiphytes, growing atop rocks, pieces of wood, and other plants and collecting moisture and nutrients from air and rainfall.) For this reason, if you want to encourage your plant to reach its mature leaf form, it's important to choose a structure with an organic surface, such as a moss pole.

Vining aroids' immature and mature forms vary so widely that they can be hard to identify—even for experts. They're often sold under the wrong name or mismatched common and scientific names. (In the guide on the following pages, we've given the correct name as well as often-seen misnomers.) No matter what you call them, these shape-shifting specimens are full of surprises.

Can't get enough of these vining plants? Turn to page 114 for the classic pothos or to chapter seven for more climbing and vining options.

LIGHT • Moderate to bright indirect light; will burn in direct sun.

WATER • Water when the top 2 inches (5 cm) of soil become dry.

HUMIDITY • Benefits from humidity.

SOIL • Well-draining potting mix amended with organic matter and orchid bark or other aggregates for added drainage, nutrition, and structure.

FERTILIZER • In the growing season (spring to fall), feed vining aroid plants a balanced or high-nitrogen liquid fertilizer once a month at half the manufacturer's recommended rate. When plant growth slows in winter, stop fertilizing.

POTTING • To climb, vining aroids require a structure with an organic surface, such as a moss pole.

PRUNING • If your vine becomes unruly, trim away leggy tendrils. This diverts energy back to growth at the crown of the plant.

PROPAGATION • Can be propagated with stem cuttings in soil or water.

VINING AROIDS

Rhaphidophora tetrasperma
'Ginny'

Though often sold as *Monstera minima*, this hardy native of Thailand and Malaysia isn't a monstera at all. It shares similarities with the monstera's immature leaf shape but develops a notably thick and sturdy upright vine. Uniformly dissected foliage, with individual leaves reaching 4 to 6 inches (10 to 15 cm) across, gives this species a uniquely graphic appeal.

Rhaphidophora decursiva
'Dragon Tail'

This sturdy and vigorous understory plant experiences a remarkable transformation on its way to maturity. Its solid, glossy leaves first develop a single deep division, taking on a quirky mitten shape. The divisions then multiply as it enters maturity, creating a palmlike appearance. 'Dragon Tail' matures faster than many vining aroids; to encourage its development, provide a moss pole where it can establish roots.

Monstera karstenianum
'Peru'

Puckered dark green veins give this monstera's foliage a complex, quilted texture. Even on young plants, the leaves appear rigid and more substantial than those of many other aroids. 'Peru' grows quickly as a vining or trailing specimen; it's equally at home in a hanging basket or on a moss pole. A relatively new arrival on the market, it's not yet widespread, but availability is increasing and prices are lowering.

Monstera adansonii
Swiss cheese vine

A popular plant in the 1970s, this vigorous vine is back in vogue thanks to its lacy leaves, each one perforated with open holes called fenestrations, which are present on both immature and mature plants. It's available in both narrow- and broad-leaved forms, depending on your style. You may sometimes see this low-maintenance species incorrectly labeled as *Monstera obliqua* or *Philodendron* 'Swiss Cheese'.

A CELEBRATION OF FORM

Once you start bringing aroids home, it's tempting to pack lots of plants into a single room for a maximalist jungle effect. But a restrained approach can be equally impactful. An edited display turns the focus to aroids' majestic overall forms, which can get lost among too many leaves. Here two highly desirable *Monstera deliciosa* 'Thai Constellation' specimens are spotlighted with minimal distractions. A stand introduces multiple levels to the display, creating a green canopy and allowing the plants—resplendent approaching full maturity—to be observed from a variety of perspectives.

To keep the focus on these exceptional specimens, we selected simple accompaniments: a matched pair of rugged pots, top-dressed with large stones to counterbalance the top-heavy structure of the monsteras. (If you top-dress your aroids, use stones or other materials sparingly; too many rocks can trap excess moisture.) When choosing vessels and accents, consider how they will tie your plants into the overall design of your space. Here the rocks echo the homeowner's stone collection on the window ledge, creating places for the eye to rest as it moves through the room.

NSE TROPICALS

PLANTATION, FLORIDA

"I've always liked weird plants," says Enid Offolter. "Different things, unusual things." Her fascination with aroids started twenty-two years ago, long before the current craze catapulted these tropicals into houseplant superstardom. Thanks to the rare specimens she grows and sells at NSE Tropicals, Enid has a reputation in the plant community that has grown as quickly as that of her beloved aroids.

Before they were her business, aroids were Enid's personal obsession. "I started buying plants on eBay for myself, and realized I could sell things there, too. Initially, it was to fund my collection; I couldn't spend money on plants unless I was making money on plants." Her eBay sales were the foundation of NSE Tropicals, but not everyone in the plant industry understood what she was doing. "There weren't many people selling plants online at all, never mind interesting ones," she says. "Older guys from the local nurseries thought it was kind of a joke. Now they're all trying to do online sales, and I get to tease them a little bit."

The aroid community was different in those days. Enid describes the enthusiasts she met early on as "science geeks, a really good group. Many of them were older, and they were excited to see a young person interested in their plants." Since aroid popularity skyrocketed around five years ago, most of her buyers are now between twenty-five and thirty-five. She's not sure what sparked the craze, but she attributes at least some of its growth to Instagram: "People can show off what they bought. When someone posts a photo of a beautiful plant, you get a hundred requests for it." She still finds parts of this meteoric rise jaw-dropping. "Some plants are the price of a car now! That's just startling to me."

The incredible demand for aroids has made NSE Tropicals into a thriving business, but Enid still

---

Though their presence is wholly practical, the misting systems used to maintain ideal moisture and humidity levels create an ethereal atmosphere in the growing spaces at NSE.

runs it by herself from her South Florida home. She estimates that she sells ten thousand plants per year, propagating them in her four shade houses, then packing and mailing them to eager houseplant enthusiasts. During busy seasons, she ships roughly 150 packages a day and still finds time to propagate one or two trays of new plants in the evening. She could hire someone to lighten her workload, but she's always preferred to run the business on her own: "When I started, I don't feel like I was taken seriously. Maybe because I was a woman, because I was only in my twenties, because I was selling online, or because rare philodendrons and anthuriums weren't as desirable then. That was okay, though. I wanted to keep my head down and do my own thing."

Things are a bit different these days. With over 100,000 Instagram followers, Enid is a celebrity in the houseplant community and often gets recognized at plant shows. In spite of the success she's had online, she has reservations about the internet's effect on plant collecting. She recalls the thrills and challenges of finding rare plants before the online sales boom: "When I started out, the Miami area had a few collectors who were the main source for plants. They had built collections over forty years of growing and trading. You might visit a grower seven times and be told that a plant wasn't for sale, then on the

eighth visit they'd decide to sell you a cutting. If you had a relationship with a botanical garden, maybe they would trade with you. Now, if you have enough money, you can get any plant online in an instant."

Change has also emerged in the way aroids are grown. Enid produces her plants via multiple types of propagation, often by seed, which promotes biodiversity but can take years. Large wholesalers, on the other hand, mass-produce plants using a method called tissue culture, essentially creating thousands of clones. These plants flood the market through big-box retailers in quantities that smaller growers can't match, often a sign that those smaller growers should shift their focus to something new and less common. "For popular plants, I've had wait lists thousands of people long. I'll never have thousands of one plant—I have more like four of everything," Enid explains.

But she understands why so many people share her passion for aroids. "Everyone wants houseplants right now, and aroids do well indoors. They come in every shape and size, from tiny 2-inch (5 cm) plants

ABOVE, LEFT: Enid and her dogs, Apollo (left) and Brutus. ABOVE, RIGHT: The fronds of a Cuban petticoat palm (*Copernicia macroglossa*). OPPOSITE: Vining aroids climb the felt substrate of a living wall, spectacular in their mature forms. Note the fenestrations that some species' leaves develop at maturity.

to up to 15 feet (4.5 m). The color range is also so broad—you can get black, green, white stripes. When I started out, there were like five aroids available. I thought, 'I have all five!' Now you have such incredible choices. There are hundreds of anthurium varieties alone!"

When asked about her favorite aroids, Enid admits that her most-loved plants don't always mirror what her customers want. She does note, however, that she thinks variegated *Philodendron gloriosum* could soon be an in-demand rarity. She's also enchanted by a *Monstera deliciosa* called 'White Monster' from Japanese grower Kunzo Nishihata,

which has otherworldly all-white leaves. (A warning to would-be collectors: it may revert, its white leaves turning green if it needs more chlorophyll to support photosynthesis.)

Enid's advice for those interested in aroids? First, join the International Aroid Society, a great source of information for new plant parents. For inspiration, she recommends two of her favorite gardens: "The Atlanta Botanical Garden is the best place to see aroids grown properly. It has a 'forest' of high-elevation, foggy-climate plants. I also love the Seattle Spheres. Their team is amazing; every person you talk to makes you smarter." Second, she suggests planning for how you'll provide an aroid with the humidity it craves *before* purchasing a plant. (See page 26 for ways to create humidity in your home.) Most of Enid's plants are grown outside thanks to the

OPPOSITE: Tropical ferns and anthuriums mingle on a living wall. ABOVE: The massive, heart-shaped leaf of *Philodendron plowmanii*.

South Florida climate, but she likes to use terrariums for humidity indoors. She notes that aroids *can* grow in lower humidity, "if you're willing to go through some crunchy leaves" during the transition from a high-humidity greenhouse to your home. "They want to grow," she says, "so they do their best."

One final thing to consider before starting an aroid collection is the ethics of collecting. Every trendy species starts as a wild plant, and unethical collection methods can put aroids and their habitats at risk. "You hope that when collectors find a plant, they take home just enough to propagate—maybe to get seeds—and grow their own," Enid says. "But with today's crazy prices, some people take everything they can from the wild and sell it. For aroids that might grow in just one specific location, if you take it all, it's gone. It's scary if those plants are going to private collectors instead of botanical gardens; if they end up with someone who can't grow them properly, they could disappear altogether."

These concerns could cast a pall over the booming business of aroids, but, Enid assures us, "lots of suppliers are doing things ethically these days—propagating from seed and growing plants out in their nurseries rather than just ripping them from the wild." (See page 35 for tips on identifying ethical sources.) Growers like these—growers like Enid— show their admiration for aroids by respecting their place in the natural world as well as the houseplant world. It's an essential outlook for the long-term survival of these fascinating plants.

ABOVE: "Right now I'm loving *Cyrtosperma hambalii*, which is native to New Guinea," says Enid. "It has leaves that resemble antlered deer heads and produces spiraling inflorescences that look like unicorn horns." RIGHT: A new *Philodendron verrucosum* leaf unfurls. OPPOSITE: Enid's outdoor growing spaces evoke her aroids' native jungle habitats. Here, a profusion of greenery frames the pathway to her primary production area.

TWO

SMALL WONDERS

PETITE & DELICATE PLANTS

NOT EVERY HOUSEPLANT NEEDS TO BE A TOWERING statement piece. The compact plants in this chapter offer a subtle type of charm that's richly detailed and well worth your attention, fitting an enormous amount of color and textural interest into a small package.

Though they hail from all corners of the plant kingdom, our petite picks share similar and approachable care needs. Their only fussy tendencies come with watering: this chapter includes members of the gesneriad family—the African violet and its cousin *Streptocarpella*. Along with cheerful flowers, all gesneriads boast fuzzy, supremely touchable leaves that are damaged by contact with water.

We particularly like to showcase small wonders on their own, so their intricate leaves and vivid blooms aren't overshadowed by larger specimens. They're outstanding as windowsill or tabletop plants because they offer lots of interest in high-traffic areas without becoming too large or unwieldy.

One more thing to love about our small-scale showstoppers: they're accessible. Most nurseries offer at least one or two varieties at a reasonable cost. They're also popular among specialty growers and hybridizers (more on that on the next page), which makes them a great introduction to collecting, because you can purchase unique species without breaking the bank. Now that we've sung the praises of these plants, let's enter their playful world with this reminder: it's all in the details.

Saintpaulia ionantha

AFRICAN VIOLET

AFRICAN VIOLETS have long been a mainstay in kitchen windows—and for good reason. They're colorful, incredibly varied, and highly collectible, and are consistent bloomers with proper care. We love their nostalgic appeal, too; beloved since Victorian times, these old-fashioned beauties offer a feminine and lighthearted counterpoint to trendy tropicals and succulents.

All African violets share two characteristics: slightly iridescent petals and plush, fuzzy leaves. Beyond that, the possibilities are endless. These petite plants are easy to hybridize, so professional growers and amateur gardeners constantly introduce new cultivars (meet one of our favorite growers on page 104). Nearly every grocery store and nursery stocks the classic flat-faced type with solid-color blooms, while specialty nurseries offer exotic ruffled petals, multicolor flowers with paint-splattered patterns, and even some highly prized yellow varieties. (Pictured here is *Saintpaulia ionantha* 'LE Green Rose'.)

Thanks to their boundless diversity, African violets are popular collector's plants. Flower shows often host novice grower competitions, and dedicated societies exist in many countries. If you're interested in collecting, these groups can connect you with nearby growers who hybridize and sell their own cultivars.

Native to higher elevations in tropical climates in eastern Africa, these violets naturally grow in nooks and crannies where they get bright indirect light throughout the day. Find yours a home on a windowsill, but protect it from midday sun. Once you've mastered the right care routine, you'll be rewarded with up to three bloom periods each year. Though they can thrive in mixed plantings with careful watering, we prefer African violets as stand-alone specimens. Enchanting in both color and texture, they need no further embellishment.

LIGHT • Bright indirect light. A north- or west-facing window in summer and an east- or south-facing window in winter is ideal. Keep away from cold glass in winter.

WATER • Maintain evenly moist, but not soggy, soil around the roots. African violets are fussy about water touching their leaves; water carefully near the roots, place the pot in a saucer of water and let moisture soak through the drainage holes, or use a self-watering pot. If leaves get wet, wipe them off and limit exposure to light to prevent spotting.

HUMIDITY • Benefits from ambient humidity.

SOIL • African violet mix.

FERTILIZER • In the growing season (spring to fall), feed with African violet–specific fertilizer or a half-strength 10-10-10 liquid houseplant fertilizer every two weeks. When plant growth slows in winter, fertilize once a month.

POTTING • African violets prefer to be slightly pot-bound. Only repot when your plant has generously outgrown its container.

PROPAGATION • Can be propagated by means of whole leaf cuttings.

Oxalis

FALSE SHAMROCK

THOUGH THEY SHARE AN ICONIC SHAPE with the three-leaf clovers you might find in your lawn, members of genus *Oxalis* are unrelated to their botanical doppelgängers (as indicated by their common name, "false shamrock"). They're part of the wood sorrel family, which includes hundreds of species across the globe.

While they vary widely in appearance, false shamrocks share a few key traits. They grow near rocky streambeds and the edges of woodland areas, so prefer dappled light and fertile, moist soil. Most have trifoliate leaves—that is, leaves divided into three leaflets—that create their instantly recognizable shape. They all grow from corms, tiny ovate food storage structures that multiply in a clump below the stems. All will flower indoors, making for a gratifying addition to their colorful foliage. Finally, many varieties are nyctinastic, meaning they open, close, and move throughout the day based on light exposure.

Members of the oxalis family are also united by an atypical growth cycle: when triggered by stressors like extreme heat, cold, or drought, they may enter dormancy—a survival technique for periods when conditions do not favor growth. If your home environment is stable throughout the year, your oxalis will continue to grow without pause. If it appears to be declining, it could be entering dormancy; though leaves will die back during this period, the corms should still be firm. (Mushy corms and blackened stems are a sign of rot, from which the plant is unlikely to recover.) A return to ideal temperature, moisture, and light conditions will encourage your oxalis to emerge from dormancy and grow again.

Though its members share the attributes above, this genus is anything but one-dimensional. For a stand-alone "pet" houseplant, choose *Oxalis triangularis* (shown here) for its nyctinastic foliage, or rosette-shaped *O. palmifrons*. For mixed plantings, try the colorful *O. adenophylla* and *O. vulcanicola* 'Molten Lava'. No matter which variety you choose, your false shamrock will stay small; mature plants generally reach no more than 5 to 10 inches (13 to 25 cm) tall. When invited inside, their modest stature and vibrant coloration make them perfect for enlivening a windowsill or desk.

LIGHT · Bright indirect light all day, or morning sun.

WATER · Water when the top inch (2.5 cm) of soil becomes dry.

HUMIDITY · Benefits from misting.

SOIL · Rich, well-draining potting mix amended with fine orchid bark for added drainage.

FERTILIZER · In the growing season (spring to fall), feed with a balanced liquid fertilizer once a month at half the manufacturer's recommended rate. When plant growth slows in winter, stop fertilizing.

PESTS & DISEASE · May be susceptible to aphids.

SHOPPING · While the clump will expand over time, an oxalis will remain relatively small overall. Buy close to the size you want to display.

PROPAGATION · During dormancy, you can divide corms from the clump and repot them to grow new plants.

PEPEROMIA

A LONGTIME STAPLE among houseplant growers, genus *Peperomia* has historically been represented by upright plants with big, round, shiny leaves. You may be familiar with the most common of these enduringly popular tropicals: *Peperomia obtusifolia*. But there's more to this genus: growers (like our friends at Harmony—see page 104) are resurfacing classics and introducing newer genetics, with a focus on fresh colors, textures, and forms. (See, for example, the *P. puteolata* pictured at left; more on this and a few of our other favorites on pages 76–77.)

Our preferred peperomia cultivars share two key characteristics: a small scale and a tendency for slow growth. Many varieties won't reach more than 12 inches (30 cm) tall at maturity, but even this takes time. Size, however, is where the similarities end. Each peperomia species differs considerably from its relatives in both care and appearance; in many cases, you'll struggle to recognize that two different peperomias are related at all. Some are leafy and delicate, others have fleshy succulent-like foliage, and still others are prized for their vibrant hues. This diversity is one of the things we love best about the genus, which has members scattered in subtropical and tropical climates around the globe. We've found that specific peperomia varieties gain popularity in different regions across the United States, so it's a delight to seek out local offerings when you travel.

As you discover new cultivars, you'll quickly learn that each one commands your attention in its own way. The incredible textures and quirky leaves of these plants draw the eye when placed on a desk, end table, or windowsill—any spot with bright indirect light where their details can be appreciated. They also excel at adding textural variation to mixed containers when paired with other specimens that can dry out between waterings, such as begonias (pages 93–99). Whether alone or anchoring a container garden, these petite and playful plants are the perfect conversation starters.

Peperomia care varies widely; be sure to research the needs of your specific plant.

LIGHT • Direct morning sun or all-day filtered indirect light.

WATER • Routine is key; avoid long periods of neglect followed by overwatering. Choose a vessel with drainage and let the soil dry between waterings. When growing, light watering once every ten to fourteen days is sufficient. In winter, water every two or three weeks.

HUMIDITY • Benefits from humidity.

SOIL • Rich, well-draining potting mix amended with fine orchid bark for added drainage.

FERTILIZER • Once a month in spring to fall, fertilize sparingly with a balanced fertilizer at half the manufacturer's recommended rate. Do not fertilize in winter.

PESTS & DISEASE • Peperomias can be susceptible to mealybugs, spider mites, and whiteflies.

SHOPPING • Peperomias are slow growing and usually sold in 4- to 6-inch (10 to 15 cm) pots. Choose a plant with rigid, upright leaves that feels full relative to the scale of its pot.

PROPAGATION • Can be propagated with stem cuttings in soil or water.

PEPEROMIA

Peperomia argyreia
Watermelon peperomia

This once-rare cultivar is now easier to find. Its teardrop leaves are striped in dark green and silver, so they look like watermelon rinds suspended from bright red stems. Though it's more finicky about under- and overwatering than other cultivars, its adorable appearance is worth the fuss.

Peperomia tetraphylla
'Hope'

This cultivar's trailing stems sprout fleshy, succulent-like leaves in groups of three or four, each one round and lightly veined. Much like angel vine (page 185), 'Hope' punctuates a space when displayed in a hanging basket or elevated container; try letting its graceful, pleasingly regular form spill from a windowsill (as seen on page 2) or shelf. This cultivar feels sturdier than other peperomias; it's also a more vigorous grower and less fussy. It's become easier to find in recent years and can be propagated in water. (See page 34 for propagation tips.)

Peperomia rotundifolia
'Ruby Cascade'

Similar in habit to succulents like string of hearts
(page 182), 'Ruby Cascade' is a low-maintenance
option for those seeking a trailing silhouette. Its slender
stems support flat, circular leaves with matte, deep green
tops and garnet red undersides. Make the most of its
coloration by suspending it in a hanging basket so you
can see the glimpses of red along each tendril.

Peperomia puteolata
'Stilt'

This sprawling plant is also called "parallel peperomia."
It produces upright stems that eventually tip into a
trailing silhouette, which becomes more exaggerated
in low-light conditions. Pointed green leaves with white
veins grow along its red stems for a study in contrast.
Its trailing shape is versatile, well suited for windowsill
planters, underplantings, and mixed plantings. It's also
a bit larger than other varieties, with stems reaching up
to 18 inches (45 cm) long; pinch back leggy stems for a
fuller, more compact shape with ample character.

Streptocarpella saxorum

STREPTOCARPELLA

THE MOST DIMINUTIVE SPECIES in this chapter when it comes to both leaves and flowers, *Streptocarpella saxorum* is also the most reliable. This dainty beauty is a workhorse that blooms nearly year-round, rewarding steady care with an abundance of flowers.

While its relative the African violet (page 70) generally produces flat-faced blooms, streptocarpella flowers are tubular with a long throat and five-lobed silhouette. Lavender or blue flowers are most common, though you can also find white varieties like 'Dancing Doves', shown here.

While its individual parts are quite small, the streptocarpella is larger in overall scale than the African violet. It has a free-branching habit and grows rapidly into a mounding form topped by cascading floral stems—a graceful shape that's perfect for display in a hanging basket or an elevated planter on a deep windowsill. We recommend choosing a larger vessel, because this prolific plant will quickly fill in any available space. Once mature, it doesn't like being moved, so choose a spot where you'll want to keep it long term.

Streptocarpella shines in highly trafficked rooms where its blooms can be enjoyed every day. We particularly love it as a vibrant centerpiece for a kitchen windowsill. It can also flourish in outdoor spaces during the summer months—consider trying a streptocarpella in a window box or hanging basket on the porch while the weather is warm. Whether you place it indoors or out, be thoughtful about location and care; like other gesneriads, these plants prefer indirect light and have particular watering requirements.

LIGHT • Bright indirect light. A northwest window protected from midday sun is ideal.

WATER • Keep the soil around the root zone evenly moist but not soggy. Streptocarpellas are fussy about water touching their leaves; water carefully near the roots, place the pot in a saucer of water and let moisture soak through the drainage holes, or use a self-watering pot. If leaves get wet, wipe them off and limit exposure to light to prevent spotting.

HUMIDITY • Benefits from ambient humidity.

SOIL • African violet mix.

FERTILIZER • In the growing season (spring to fall), feed with a balanced liquid fertilizer every two weeks. When plant growth slows in winter, fertilize once a month.

POTTING • Repot every spring.

PRUNING • Prune away spent flower stalks and leggy branches for a fuller, more compact look.

PROPAGATION • You can divide your plant during repotting; if you see multiple stems sprouting from the soil, break apart the root-ball and repot each section separately.

A NOD TO NOSTALGIA

When showcasing small and delicate specimens, lean into their nostalgic appeal by hearkening back to the windowsill collections of decades past. These groupings provide a cheery infusion of color and texture, along with ever-changing points of interest. A consistent scale unites the assortment of streptocarpella, African violets, and *Oxalis vulcanicola* shown here, but contrasting hues and leaf shapes enliven the display. Many of these plants bloom year-round or intermittently throughout the year.

As you curate a collection of petite plants, seek opportunities to introduce additional layers of interest. Here, terra-cotta pots visually unify the group while simultaneously playing up its nostalgic nature with traditional silhouettes. Because each specimen is so small and intricate, placement is key. Choose a location like the windowsill above your kitchen sink, where you'll be able to approach and interact with these specimens every day.

THREE

POP ART

COLORFUL & HIGHLY PATTERNED PLANTS

THESE PLANTS ARE SHOW-OFFS, AND WE MEAN THAT AS A compliment. Each specimen on the following pages possesses foliage with a treasure trove of arresting features—vivid hues, exotic variegations, touchable surfaces, and graphic forms. While most houseplants are chosen for the interest provided by their overall appearance, these specialize in smaller details. Each individual leaf is rich in color, pattern, and shape, offering the opportunity to create highly specific and layered displays that complement your decor.

Though their foliage commands your attention, these plants are undemanding in other respects. Most squeeze lots of excitement into moderately sized silhouettes, so they won't overwhelm a space. All are tropical forest natives that thrive in indirect light, saving your precious window real estate for more finicky specimens. They do require a consistent watering routine and ample drainage, so they're a great fit for intermediate gardeners.

Once their needs are met, these plants are a designer's dream come true. If your houseplant collection feels too uniform, they provide an instant change of pace: a chartreuse, hot pink, or black punctuation mark in a sea of green foliage. One outstanding plant can also function as a distinctive interior design element. Imagine, for example, a cluster of spindly cane begonias (such as *Begonia luxurians*, page 95) in a sleek modern space, or a riotously patterned calathea (page 87) taking the place of artwork in a neutral room. Though impactful enough to stand on their own, they're even more delightful when showcased together. And that's a good thing, because you'll find it impossible to bring just one of these colorful personalities home.

CTENANTHE 'GOLDEN MOSAIC'

A HARDER-TO-FIND RELATIVE of calathea and maranta—which you'll encounter later in this chapter—ctenanthe shares several qualities with its more familiar cousins. It's a shade-loving native of tropical Central and South America, where it grows on the forest floor. Like maranta and calathea, it may be nyctinastic; many varieties of ctenanthe have leaves that open in the morning and close at night. It stands out from its relatives, however, in two ways: its foliage and its size.

First, let's talk foliage. Ctenanthes have ovate leaves with squared-off edges, each one poised atop a long, slender stem. While rainbow hues from classic green to silver and red are available, we'll spotlight one impressive cultivar: *Ctenanthe lubersii* 'Golden Mosaic'. It's our favorite thanks to its eye-catching variegation; each prominently veined, matte green leaf is painted with irregular creamy yellow markings. No two leaves are alike, giving the plant an air of unpredictability that brightens any room.

This vibrant cultivar will thrive in almost any room, too, because ctenanthes are generally hardy and reliable. They can tolerate lower-light conditions, making them a favorite among home growers and designers with challenging spaces. They do require humidity and regular watering but will tell you if their needs aren't met by displaying wilted or browning leaves. Most important, they're sturdy enough to recover if you rectify the issue in time.

An outlier among the compact species in this chapter, 'Golden Mosaic' offers splashy color at floor-plant scale, reaching around 3 feet (0.9 m) tall and 4 feet (1.2 m) wide. Its long leaves grow in horizontal planes, creating an elegant, layered effect as the plant becomes established. Its upright form is stately rather than sprawling, and its well-defined horizontal lines draw the eye, offering a visual resting place in busy spaces. Think of it as a tropical oasis: a colorful moment of calm with an impactful presence.

LIGHT • Moderate indirect light; can't tolerate full sun.

WATER • Keep the soil consistently moist, particularly during periods of growth. Ctenanthes are sensitive to chlorine, so use distilled water, or leave tap water out for twenty-four hours so the chlorine evaporates. Crispy leaf edges indicate chlorine damage.

HUMIDITY • Benefits from humidity; you may see leaves curl or develop brown tips if humidity is too low.

SOIL • Rich, well-draining potting mix.

FERTILIZER • In the growing season (spring to fall), feed with a balanced liquid fertilizer every two weeks. When plant growth slows in winter, stop fertilizing.

PESTS & DISEASE • Can be susceptible to spider mites and mealybugs.

SHOPPING • You may occasionally see ctenanthe called "never never plant," though this name is less common than it once was. Ctenanthes grow at a moderate pace, so they're most often sold at larger sizes; you'll find them in 8-inch (20 cm) pots or larger. That said, they've become less available in recent years, so purchase whatever size you can find!

CALATHEA

CALATHEAS ARE INCREDIBLY DIVERSE in appearance and widely available at almost any nursery, a winning combination for those seeking novel hues, textures, and patterns. A recent explosion of showy cultivars has made these tropicals more collectible than ever—the hardest part is deciding which one to buy first.

No matter your taste or design goals, there's a calathea for you. Pictured at right is the *Calathea orbifolia*—learn more about this and three of our other favorite varieties on the following pages. The sprawling genus ranges from long, strappy leaves to softly rounded forms; glossy rigid surfaces to touchable velvet textures; and deep greens to splashes of shocking pink. (This group contains arguably the most striking pink houseplants we've ever seen!) Most have leaves with red-tinted undersides, creating a delightful tricolor effect in variegated specimens. The leaves emerge as tiny tubes, unfurl in entrancing whorls, then perch atop individual stems for a silhouette that's unusual among houseplants: simultaneously full and airy.

Those broad leaves have lots of surface area to catch sunlight, so calatheas thrive anywhere with a reasonable amount of indirect light, saving precious window space for sun-loving specimens. Some varieties are nyctinastic, so you'll see their leaves open and close in response to light each day. These tropical natives of Central and South America are somewhat particular about watering and humidity, but that can be a rewarding challenge for those looking to hone their skills.

One other thing to love about the calathea: it's bold but not overbearing. While its cousin maranta (page 90) has a rambling shape suited to hanging baskets and tabletop planters, the calathea is more upright, offering a look that's dense yet compact in overall stature. Larger plants make modestly sized floor specimens, while petite plants are perfect on a desk or side table. A classic houseplant for good reason, every calathea packs lots of personality into a small package.

LIGHT • Indirect light; can't tolerate full sun.

WATER • Keep the soil generally moist, letting the top 2 inches (5 cm) dry out between waterings. Calatheas are sensitive to chlorine and cold water; use room-temperature distilled water, or leave tap water out for twenty-four hours so the chlorine evaporates. Crispy leaf edges indicate chlorine damage.

HUMIDITY • Patchy leaf edges indicate too little water or humidity.

SOIL • Well-draining potting mix amended with organic matter and fine orchid bark or other aggregates for added drainage and nutrition.

FERTILIZER • In the growing season (spring to fall), feed with a balanced liquid fertilizer every two weeks. When plant growth slows in winter, stop fertilizing. After repotting, give the roots time to recover before fertilizing.

TEMPERATURE • Avoid drastic temperature variations, cold drafts, and doorways.

PESTS & DISEASE • Calatheas can be susceptible to spider mites.

SHOPPING • You may see calatheas labeled as "prayer plants"; for the true prayer plant, see page 90.

POTTING • These moderate growers tolerate becoming pot-bound.

CALATHEA

Goeppertia kegeljanii

Musaica

This harder-to-find species (previously known as *Calathea musaica*, which is how you'll often still see it sold) is prized for its jaw-dropping, mosaiclike geometric pattern (which inspired its name). Though understated in color, the lancelike leaves are entrancingly ornamental, like nature's answer to stained glass.

Calathea orbifolia

This species' new growth emerges in vivacious chartreuse, maturing to minty green with even lighter stripes. Broad, rounded leaves fan outward from its center, forming a lofty canopy. Pronounced veins add ample texture, while the silvery hue makes a sophisticated counterpoint to brighter foliage.

Calathea
'White Fusion'

An especially dense growth habit sets this cultivar apart from other calatheas, but impressionistic variegation is its most appealing trait. Each leaf is patterned with splashes of soft blush, while the undersides are a delicate pinkish lavender.

Calathea
'Royal Standard'

We love this variety for its upright and arching silhouette, which is uncommon among calatheas. Its foliage is also quite colorful; each leaf features a silver face, painterly dark green margins, and a soft mauve underside.

Maranta leuconeura 'Lemon Lime'

MARANTA 'LEMON LIME'

LIGHT • Indirect light; can't tolerate full sun. Too much direct light will weaken the color.

WATER • Keep the soil generally moist; let it dry slightly between waterings. Marantas are sensitive to chlorine, so use distilled water, or leave tap water out for twenty-four hours so the chlorine can evaporate. Crispy leaf edges indicate chlorine damage.

HUMIDITY • Though they can't tolerate overwatering, marantas benefit from humidity.

SOIL • Rich, well-draining potting mix.

FERTILIZER • In the growing season (spring to fall), feed with a balanced liquid fertilizer every two weeks. When plant growth slows in winter, stop fertilizing.

PESTS & DISEASE • Reliable movement is a sign of good health; if you notice that your maranta has stopped moving, look for watering or pest issues. In lower humidity, spider mites or mealybugs can become a problem.

PRUNING • Maranta plants respond well to pruning; you can trim back rangy stems to achieve a tighter shape and encourage denser new growth. (This is also a good time to take cuttings for propagation.)

PROPAGATION • Can be propagated with stem cuttings in soil or water.

THE MARANTA knows a remarkable party trick: it moves. Native to tropical Central and South America, it's commonly called the "prayer plant" because it is nyctinastic, meaning its leaves unfurl to capture daylight, then draw shut at night in a slow-motion gesture that resembles hands being brought together in prayer—an adaptation that preserves water.

While this restless nature is the maranta's most unusual feature, there's more to appreciate about its flashy foliage. Marantas are beloved for their iconic leaves, which are oval, deeply veined, and available in several saturated hues. Our favorite cultivar is 'Lemon Lime', whose dark green foliage is punctuated by high-contrast chartreuse markings. It's also easy to find solid green specimens as well as *Maranta leuconeura* 'Erythroneura', sold as "red maranta," which features hot pink veins against a deep green backdrop.

A maranta is the perfect step up if you've had success with a pothos (page 114) and want something similarly lush and significantly more intriguing, if slightly more challenging in terms of care. At a mature height of 12 to 14 inches (30 to 36 cm), these tropicals are manageable in size but love to ramble, sprouting lateral branches before gaining height in spurts. New growth is clumpy and often asymmetrical, creating layers of foliage with each leaf perched perkily atop its stem. The branches form a dense, vase-shaped silhouette that's filled with personality, further enlivened by the continuously shifting leaves. Place your maranta in a humid bathroom, in a hanging basket or tabletop planter, making sure it has room to spread out so you can enjoy its ever-changing appearance. Part plant and part tiny creature, it has a mind of its own.

CANE BEGONIA

WE WOULD BE REMISS IN CURATING a chapter on color without mentioning begonias. Though when you hear "begonia" you may think of waxy-leaved grocery store staples, this dazzling genus is far more diverse. So diverse, in fact, that we've broken it into two subgroups: cane begonias and rhizomatous begonias (page 96), both of which contain tropical natives prized for their extraordinary foliage and distinctive forms. While equally adept at adding character to indoor gardens, each group offers its own set of design opportunities.

If you want statement foliage with lofty ambitions, look no further than cane begonias. These stately plants are named for their tall, upright stems, which resemble bamboo canes and sprout leaves in dramatic shapes and hues. These leaves take myriad forms, from deeply textured palmate silhouettes that sprawl 2 feet (0.6 m) across (*Begonia* 'Paul Hernandez') to fuzzy, heart-shaped cups (*B. venosa* 'White Rhino', shown at right). Turn the page for more on these and two of our other favorite varieties.

Some of the best-known cultivars are classic "angel wing" types, topped by elongated and fluttery leaves. Though foliage is the main attraction, cane begonias also bloom, producing clusters of flowers—a charming flourish for an already-fascinating plant.

Some cane begonias grow to substantial heights and are large enough to serve as floor plants; others are more compact but no less rich in color and texture. With so many uncommon features to appreciate, these begonias can easily stand on their own, but they're at their best among friends in a grouping of potted plants. Wherever you display your cane begonia, it will be a stunning centerpiece for your collection—shapely, vibrant, and playfully exuberant.

LIGHT • Bright indirect light. Rotate plants a quarter turn every two weeks to maintain even growth.

WATER • Water when the surface of the soil is dry to the touch. Begonias rot quickly in waterlogged soil, so avoid overwatering.

HUMIDITY • Cane begonias thrive in ambient humidity. Crispy leaf edges indicate that humidity is too low.

SOIL • Well-draining potting mix amended with organic matter and orchid bark or other aggregates for added drainage, nutrition, and support.

FERTILIZER • Cane begonias bloom from summer into fall; promote prolonged flower production with light weekly feedings with a balanced liquid fertilizer at half the manufacturer's recommended rate. Once flowering is complete, reduce feeding to just once a month.

SHOPPING • Select full plants with rigid leaves. Overwatered plants have mushy leaves and/or browning near the crown and should be avoided.

PROPAGATION • In general, begonia plants are not long lived and require renewal through propagation. They are, however, exceptionally easy to propagate. If a branch breaks off, pop it in water and it will grow roots!

CANE BEGONIA

Begonia
'Paul Hernandez'

This exuberant cultivar is a bona fide statement maker, with broad palmate leaves that reach 24 inches (61 cm) across. Deep green with a pinkish red underside, each pendulous leaf has a craggy, crinkled texture, giving the plant a prehistoric look. Six feet (1.8 m) tall and equally wide at maturity, it's a fantastic floor plant for larger spaces.

Begonia amphioxus

Native to Malaysia, this species is truly a shrub begonia, but it offers the habit and standout foliage of an angel wing at a smaller scale. Maxing out at 18 inches (46 cm) tall, *B. amphioxus* has tiny yet eye-catching leaves, each one frilly and scattered with red polka dots. This petite plant can be tricky to care for; it craves humidity, so is often happiest in a terrarium or cloche. Bright indirect light and a well-drained, slightly acidic soil are also essential for this challenging yet rewarding specimen.

Begonia luxurians

Begonia venosa
'White Rhino'

Packed with character, this tree-shaped species produces palmate, umbrellalike leaves atop slender stems. Reddish stems and glossy green foliage give *B. luxurians* a fantastically high-contrast look. Though the leaves become denser as the plant matures, it remains narrow overall. Mature specimens can reach 8 feet (2.4 m) tall but are easily pruned to a more modest size.

This cultivar is distinctive among caning types, cloaked in gently cupped, heart-shaped leaves. The hazy silver-green foliage has a fuzzy texture that's more prominent in new growth. It's more compact and feminine than other members of the group, reaching just 16 to 24 inches (40 to 61 cm) tall. 'White Rhino' benefits from more water and direct sun than most cane begonias—try a space with morning sunlight.

RHIZOMATOUS BEGONIA

LIGHT • Bright indirect light.

WATER • Water when the surface of the soil is dry to the touch. Begonias will rot quickly in waterlogged soil.

HUMIDITY • While rhizomatous begonias appreciate humidity, too much direct misting can cause mildew. They prefer ambient humidity. Crispy leaf edges indicate that the humidity is too low.

SOIL • Well-draining potting mix amended with organic matter and fine orchid bark or other aggregates for added drainage and nutrition.

FERTILIZER • From spring to summer, lightly feed with a balanced liquid fertilizer once a month at half the manufacturer's recommended rate. In fall and winter, fertilize once every month and a half to two months.

SHOPPING • Select full plants with rigid leaves. Overwatered plants have mushy leaves and/or browning near the crown; avoid these.

PROPAGATION • In general, begonia plants are not long lived. They are, however, easy to propagate. If a branch breaks off, pop it in water and it will grow roots! You can also propagate via whole leaf cuttings.

WELCOME TO THE CANDY STORE of the plant world. An enormously diverse genus group, rhizomatous begonias are available in endless permutations of color, texture, and pattern, with a tendency for ornamentation around their leaves' veins and margins. Ranging from graphic to painterly, their vibrant foliage features watercolor swirls, three-dimensional corkscrews, chartreuse freckles, and iridescent velvety surfaces that shine in mix-and-match groupings. Pictured at left is 'Harmony's Witchy Woman'; learn more about this and three more of our favorite specimens on pages 98–99.

While you may not be familiar with rhizomatous begonias, you'll likely recognize the enduringly popular rex begonia. All rex begonias are rhizomatous, but not all rhizomatous begonias are rex types. Rex or not, all rhizomatous begonias (as their name suggests) spread via rhizomes, subterranean stems that sprout roots and shoots. In addition, all rhizomatous begonias share a similar habit: a clumping, low-profile silhouette that contrasts sharply with upright cane begonias (page 93).

This compact habit, in turn, means rhizomatous begonias' design opportunities are as diverse as their appearances. They excel as tabletop or hanging-basket plants and in underplantings. They also make a wonderful warm-weather addition to outdoor living spaces. Use them as an unexpected element to brighten a patio, porch, or window box during the summer months, then bring them inside for winter color.

RHIZOMATOUS BEGONIA

Begonia
'Harmony's Witchy Woman'

A relatively easy-to-find statement piece, this cultivar from the begonia experts at Harmony (see page 104) displays the spiraling growth pattern common among traditional rex types. Its large leaves are pointy and heavily serrated with ruffled edges, a texture that's particularly beguiling on new growth. Vivid coloration adds further interest; deep red margins frame a pale green interior, returning to red near the center of the leaf.

Begonia
'Zumba'

This charming cultivar's loose spiral leaves feature ruddy brown details atop a vivid chartreuse base. The dark patterning follows the veins in each leaf for an intriguingly intricate look. It also has a shorter, denser habit, with clusters of smaller leaves, compared to the other cultivars shown here.

Begonia

'Harmony's Shooting Star'

Another stunning rex begonia from Harmony
(see page 104), we love this plant for its massive
leaves, which can reach 10 to 11 inches (25 to 28 cm)
 wide. Silver splotches decorate each leaf in a celestial
pattern, turning pink where they intersect with the
dark maroon margins. This unfussy cultivar is similar in
structure to 'Harmony's Witchy Woman', boasting spiral-
shaped leaves finished with finely fringed edges.

Begonia

'Marmaduke'

This medium-size rhizomatous begonia (18 inches/45 cm
tall at maturity) is crowned by a dome of large, oak-like
leaves with undulating margins. Each leaf is mottled in
hot chartreuse and purplish brown; on some plants the
pattern is well defined, on others quite hazy. Combined
with a rippling, craggy leaf surface and fuzzy hairs
dusting its stems and foliage, 'Marmaduke' is a riot of
color and texture.

WATERMELON BEGONIA

PROCRIS REPENS—also sold as *Pellionia pulchra*—is neither a watermelon nor a begonia, but your first glance at this plant's foliage will make the inspiration for its common name clear. Its heavily veined, begonia-like leaves are marbled with high-contrast variegations, creating a look that's reminiscent of a watermelon rind. You can find watermelon begonia cultivars in a range of colors, from deep green to dark purple to nearly black. All share a matte finish, and some have pinkish stems, a vivid finishing touch. The leaves alone make *P. repens* irresistible, but there's more to love about this vigorous and vibrant plant.

For starters, its habit is just as captivating as its foliage. The watermelon begonia's pinnate leaves are staggered along each trailing stem, extending outward to create a flattened silhouette. The stems themselves form an arched mound as they grow, tumbling downward in a bold profusion of pattern. Though it needs no further embellishment, *P. repens* also produces petite, pale pink bracts topped with white flowers (similar in appearance to true begonias). These flowers are a small but sweet flourish atop the showstopping foliage.

In its native Southeast Asia, *P. repens* grows as an understory plant. At home, it's best displayed in a way that showcases its cascading shape; pair it with a hanging basket or an urn, or place it on a ledge or shelf. This humidity lover is great for a bathroom or a terrarium, where it will flourish in the moisture-rich air. In a terrarium, try providing it with an organic surface like a plank of wood; the leaves will "shingle," attaching to the wood and climbing for a vertical display. Whether utilized as a trailer or climber, the watermelon begonia adds an attention-grabbing pop of pattern to any houseplant collection.

LIGHT • Bright to moderate indirect light; can handle partial sun (morning sun or east-facing window). Color will be more intense with some direct exposure, but droopy or brown leaf tips indicate too much sun.

WATER • Water when the top inch (2.5 cm) of soil is dry. Don't let it dry out completely.

HUMIDITY • Requires humidity and will become stressed in dry environments. Brown or drooping leaf tips indicate a lack of humidity.

SOIL • Rich, well-draining potting mix.

FERTILIZER • In the growing season (spring to fall), feed with a balanced liquid fertilizer every two weeks at half the manufacturer's recommended rate. Your plant may rest in winter, but if it is still growing, fertilize once a month.

TEMPERATURE • *P. repens* is easily stressed by cold drafts, which can cause leaves to droop or brown at the tips.

PESTS & DISEASE • Susceptible to mealybugs and aphids.

SHOPPING • Typically sold in 6- to 8-inch (15 to 20 cm) hanging baskets. It's a less common find, usually offered by hobbyists or only in small batches from growers.

PROPAGATION • Can be propagated via partial leaf cutting.

NATURE'S PALETTE

With such character and variety in appearance, the specimens in this chapter offer the opportunity to be particularly intentional about using plants as decor. While each of these varieties is a stylish conversation piece on its own, we find them most striking in groups, where their brilliant hues, hypnotic patterns, and bold shapes come alive through contrast.

In this grouping (from left to right: *Maranta leuconeura* var. *kerchoveana*, *Goeppertia majestica* 'White Star', *Goeppertia ornata*, *Calathea orbifolia*, *Ctenanthe setosa* 'Grey Star', *Goeppertia warscewiczii*), pattern takes center stage. Crisply striped leaves in a variety of scales provide a layer of graphic interest against the simple color blocking of the home's woodwork. A tonal foliage palette plays a supporting role, its rich greens enlivened by recurring flourishes of rosy hues.

HARMONY FOLIAGE

SORRENTO, FLORIDA

As Deb Cox tells it, she and her partner, Robin Jordan, didn't set out to be the leading growers of African violets and begonias—they just have a knack for seizing opportunities. Their love affair with plants started in the early 1980s, when Robin went to work at what was then called Harmony Foliage Farm. In 1987, she took over and started leasing their greenhouses; Deb soon joined her full-time, and they purchased the business in 1990. Thirty years later, Harmony Foliage is synonymous with the industry's most innovative hybrids.

"It took us a while to find where we fit," Deb says of their early years. "We started out growing mostly philodendrons, plus a few African violets and begonias. Then a storm devastated our greenhouses in 1993. It was hard, but it was the best thing that could have happened." The old greenhouses were designed for philodendrons, but Robin and Deb rebuilt with violets and begonias in mind—a business that expanded when they reached another crossroads.

"Shortly after the storm, our begonia supplier retired," Deb says. "To maintain quality, we started growing our own. Like the storm, it felt awful but changed everything." Harmony's future was shaped by one more unexpected opportunity: a fateful meeting with a member of the local African violet club. "We'd been frustrated for a while with the quality of the violets we were buying, and a member of the club offered to bring us leaves from their best violets—not commercial plants, collector stuff. Once we started propagating from those leaves, we controlled our destiny. We could manage the quality and varieties we wanted to grow."

Harmony's beautifully aged greenhouses reflect the decades that Deb and Robin have spent growing their business. To the left of the doors, mature angel wing begonia mother plants form a hedge around the perimeter.

Over time, Harmony became known for exclusive plants. They credit their success to relationships with collectors, including Charles Jaros. "He was our first begonia contact, a huge part of our education, and a great friend," Deb says. Charles introduced them to fellow collector Mary Sizemore. Both world travelers, Charles and Mary brought back violets and begonias from tropical and subtropical countries like Malaysia and Ecuador. Thus began a mutually beneficial relationship that continues today: collectors bring their latest finds to Harmony, where they're cultivated and distributed so more collectors can enjoy them. (See more on ethical sourcing on page 35.)

From the rare plants in Deb and Robin's greenhouses, more opportunities emerged. Harmony's signature African violets all started as "sports," an industry term for spontaneous mutations that occur as new plants grow. Deb spotted the splashy leaves of what would eventually be named *Saintpaulia* 'Harmony's Little Stinker', now a world-famous variety, in a tray of plants from Canada. "We were like, 'Oh my God, what is that?' Our earliest varieties started with selecting what was interesting to us and working with it—not shipping our unusual sports out the door."

African violets were Harmony's claim to fame for years. That changed in 2016, when they began hybridizing begonias. To understand the shift, it's important to know how these plants grow. Begonias and African violets are propagated by means of

---

ABOVE: 'Harmony's Fire Woman', a rex begonia. OPPOSITE, TOP: Deb (left) and Robin among their rex begonias. OPPOSITE, BOTTOM: The leaves and flowers of 'Harmony's Quasimodo', an angel wing begonia.

"wedge cutting": a grower snips wedges from a leaf, then roots them in a mist bed until plantlets emerge. African violets are slow and labor intensive, taking up to six months from mother leaf to viable plant. Begonias grow faster, which promotes the emergence of more sports. Those sports, in turn, can be used to create new hybrids—a project that has become Deb's chief passion.

Harmony's first hybrid started with a show-stopping "dragon wing" begonia sport. Deb says, "We were equally invested in violets and begonias until that point, but we couldn't ignore that sport. We'd considered partnering with hybridizers before, but when we saw that dragon wing, we decided to do it ourselves. How hard could it be?"

Hybridization involves pollinating the female bloom of one plant (like a favorite sport) with pollen collected from the male bloom of another, letting the

seedpod dry, sowing the seeds . . . and waiting. Each pod produces thousands of plants, so Deb and Robin must wait until they mature to see the results, test their performance, and make selections. It can take two years to achieve a distinct hybrid.

Unlike the search for sports, hybridizing is methodical and multifaceted. Deb describes it as "making educated decisions about what to cross and the desired outcome." She continues, "Our years as growers give us insight as to what will get the right results. Harmony hybrids aren't all about looks: they're also tested to be sure they won't fail in summer heat or go dormant in winter. We're not just working on crazy shapes but toward a begonia that holds its color in summer, which is a big deal in Florida. We've also been developing an angel wing to outshine *Begonia maculata* var. *wightii*—a big, spotted variety that's a good grower."

The looks, however, are spectacular. Their first begonia hybrid, 'Harmony's Fire Breathing Dragon', triggered an explosion of both dragon wings and angel wings, whose imaginative names reflect their exotic appearances. Deb cites 'Harmony's Icicles', 'Harmony's

OPPOSITE: Deb holds a massive mother plant of *Begonia barsalouxiae*, a rhizomatous species. ABOVE: Among African violet enthusiasts, Harmony is known for the name tags that they place on their plants. (While most growers don't provide varietal names, Deb and Robin give them for all their violets.)

Bat Out of Hell', and 'Harmony's Bird of Prey' as recent standouts—her excitement builds as she describes them: "We're getting so many unique shapes! 'Bat Out of Hell' and 'Bird of Prey' are angel wings that will change the hybridizing landscape. I'm already crossing them—can't wait to see what we get!"

Near the end of our conversation, we return to Deb and Robin's early years and how it felt to enter the male-dominated plant industry as a lesbian couple. Looking back, they believe the quality of their plants made it possible. Deb says, "We were young when we started, and this part of Florida was pretty backward. But once people saw our product was good, it wasn't a struggle. I remember the first time we loaded our truck with samples and went around to all the brokers. If our product hadn't been good, we would have been 'those girls that grow bad plants.' Instead, we became the girls at Harmony. We weren't really out, but we weren't hiding—being women was a bigger deal. When our brokers called, they'd ask, 'What did you girls do this weekend? How did you spend the holiday?' It just wasn't a thing."

It's hard to imagine retirement for this pioneering duo, but the subject looms large as they enter their sixties. One thing is certain: they won't let their hard work fade away. "It keeps me awake at night," Deb admits. "We're committed to finding someone to carry on our legacy. And, hopefully, who will let me come to the greenhouse and hybridize!"

When it comes to hybridizing, angel wing begonias—like 'Harmony's Flying High', seen here—are Deb's biggest focus. A newer variety, 'Harmony's Bird of Prey', is her current favorite: "I can't walk into the greenhouse without going to visit it."

FOUR

UNFUSSY FRIENDS

LOW-LIGHT & LOW-MAINTENANCE

PROBLEM SOLVERS

FOR THOSE FOLKS JUST SPROUTING A GREEN THUMB, low-maintenance plants are key for developing the skills and confidence needed to cultivate more-challenging varieties. They're also the perfect match for those who know their limitations. Whether you're a frequent traveler whose unpredictable schedule disrupts complex care routines, an overzealous waterer, or simply someone prone to forgetfulness, these tough-to-kill plants can withstand neglect—and look surprisingly stylish while doing it.

Easygoing plants also have an important role as problem solvers for challenging spaces. They make it possible to introduce greenery in dark, dry, or drafty rooms where more particular houseplants would quickly decline.

These plants, however, aren't just practical workhorses. They're also aesthetic charmers with sculptural shapes, vivid colors, and varied sizes (options featured in this chapter include a low-light indoor tree). If you've searched for easy houseplants before, some of the names you encounter here may be familiar. Many are impressive enough for display as a stand-alone specimen—even if you've cultivated a collection of more exotic plants. Finding the perfect balance between practicality and beauty, our unfussy friends make it rewardingly simple to invite plants into your home.

POTHOS

POTHOS reigned as a popular houseplant in the 1970s; in the decades since, it has become a common sight atop kitchen cabinets, lofty perches that leave room for its long, leafy stems. This close relative of the philodendron (page 42) is a staple thanks to its tolerance for limited light and moisture. Vigorous, cheerful, and miraculously healthy with minimal care, it's the perfect no-fuss plant.

In fact, a pothos's only weakness is *too much* fuss; it struggles with overwatering and desires a consistent routine. That makes it ideal for hard-to-reach places like high shelves or cabinet tops—you won't need to worry about climbing up with your watering can too often! Such settings also offer the indirect light that a pothos craves; these natives of Southeast Asia and Australia are understory plants, adapted to sunlight filtered through the forest above.

Though these plants are climbers in the wild, you'll likely see them as trailing houseplants. Each stem supports a cascade of spade-shaped leaves, offering draping and movement for a look that stands out among the upright shapes of other low-maintenance plants. An elevated location like a pedestal or shelf makes the most of this silhouette.

Note: These plants were formerly classified under the genus *Pothos*, which remains their most frequently used common name. They have, however, been classified and reclassified, so you may see cultivars sold under various scientific names—look for *Scindapsus*, *Epipremnum*, and *Philodendron*. Turn the page for a closer look at some of our favorites, which offer everything from high-contrast variegation to a cool silver-blue hue, such as that of the *Epipremnum pinnatum* 'Cebu Blue' pictured at left.

One final note about these classic houseplants—they're also among the easiest to propagate so you can grow more of your favorite varieties. If you love the look of pothos and feel ready for more challenging care requirements, head to chapter seven to level up with additional vining houseplants.

LIGHT • Indirect light.

WATER • Water only when the soil is completely dry. Some leaf drop as the plant ages is normal; losing many leaves at once can indicate overwatering. Inconsistent watering can cause rangy growth.

HUMIDITY • Benefits from humidity.

SOIL • Well-draining potting mix; you may wish to amend with organic matter and orchid bark or other aggregates for added drainage, nutrition, and structure.

FERTILIZER • In the growing season (spring to fall), feed with a balanced liquid fertilizer once a month at half the manufacturer's recommended rate. When plant growth slows in winter, stop fertilizing.

PESTS & DISEASE • Pothos can be susceptible to mealybugs; premature leaf drop is often an indicator of infestation.

SHOPPING • Look for full plants with upright, sturdy stems.

PRUNING • Pothos plants benefit from regular trimming. Prune lanky stems for a compact, fuller plant.

PROPAGATION • Can be propagated with stem cuttings in soil or water.

POTHOS

Epipremnum pinnatum
'Cebu Blue'

Epipremnum aureum
'Global Green'

Also sold as *Philodendron* 'Cebu Blue', this plant has an unusual and alluring hue. Emerging a glaucous silver-blue, the immature leaves are lance-shaped and petite (around 3 inches/8 cm long) with well-defined veins. Mature leaves are a vibrant green and heavily dissected, but most home growers won't see this evolution. Unless *E. pinnatum* is given the time and climbing space to reach a very large size (10 to 14 feet/3 to 4 m), the leaves will remain immature—and blue!

Pothos varieties with green-on-green variegations are gaining popularity, offering a counterpoint to the higher-contrast variegated cultivars. This newer option is a vivid take on the trend; its leaves feature chartreuse centers and irregular, dark green margins. With a slightly crinkled texture, 'Global Green' is also a departure from the pothos's classic smooth-leaf look.

Scindapsus pictus
'Jade Satin'

This solid green variety seems simple at first glance, but a closer look reveals hidden depths. A subtle twist on the enduringly popular jade pothos, 'Jade Satin' has foliage with a matte finish that lends it a soft, dreamy texture. Its leaves—which are larger than average for a pothos—gain additional dimension from an intricate network of veins.

Epipremnum pinnatum
'Marble Queen'

This older variety is a standby in the market—and for good reason. Its high-color white-and-green variegation is nuanced and feathery, with irregular markings so fine that they resemble a snowstorm. Bright but not distracting, it's a great choice for enlivening a darker space, since (like all pothos plants) it's low maintenance and tolerant of limited light.

Aspidistra elatior 'Milky Way'

CAST-IRON PLANT 'MILKY WAY'

YOU MAY KNOW *ASPIDISTRA ELATIOR* by one of its evocative common names: "cast-iron plant" or "barroom plant." It has a well-earned reputation for being incredibly hard to kill; it's as tough as nails and can handle the rigors of life in a dark bar corner—including a spilled beer or two. If you have a low-light space and a tendency to forget about watering, this plant is ready to roll with the punches. While the solid green variety is a classic houseplant, we're enchanted by an unusually patterned option: *A. elatior* 'Milky Way'.

'Milky Way' is one of several exotic *Aspidistra* cultivars that can be found in the market. Its dark green leaves are speckled with small white dots, creating a celestial appearance that inspires its name. This stunner is (pardon the pun) stellar at brightening low-light and low-traffic spaces, such as a rarely used guest room. Native to forest understories on islands of East Asia, it tolerates very limited light and has minimal watering needs, so it's perfectly okay with being forgotten. You may, however, find yourself visiting those neglected areas more often to enjoy your plant!

The cast-iron plant is a member of the asparagus family, but it looks more like an overgrown lily of the valley without the flowers. Its flexible leaves grow in an upright clump, which reaches 2 to 3 feet (60 to 90 cm) tall and 1 to 3 feet (30 to 90 cm) wide at maturity. *A. elatior* spreads via rhizomes, eventually filling in its container with full, bushy foliage. Its mature size is fairly modest, yet its abundant and intricately patterned leaves make 'Milky Way' a plant with presence.

While it will become denser over time, *A. elatior* is quite slow growing. Combined with limited availability in the current houseplant market, this can make it rather expensive. You may experience some sticker shock when shopping, but don't be put off by the price. This plant is an eye-catching investment piece that's nearly impossible to kill, so you'll enjoy its starry presence for years to come.

LIGHT • Low to moderate indirect light. Tolerates full shade; do not expose to direct sun.

WATER • Water only when the soil is completely dry.

SOIL • Rich, well-draining potting mix.

FERTILIZER • In the growing season (spring to fall), feed with a balanced liquid fertilizer once a month at half the manufacturer's recommended rate. When plant growth slows in winter, stop fertilizing.

PESTS & DISEASE • *Aspidistra elatior* is susceptible to spider mites and root rot. Watch for yellow spots on the leaves, which can indicate fungal root rot caused by overwatering.

SHOPPING • Though its popularity has waned in the last ten to fifteen years, we think this species is close to a resurgence. It's a rare find for now, so purchase at any size. Since they're slow growing, you may see plants in 8- to 10-inch (20 to 25 cm) pots that have fewer leaves than expected for their scale. Don't worry—your specimen will become fuller over time.

LIGHT • Low indirect light is sufficient. Can tolerate bright indirect light; avoid full sun.

WATER • Water every few weeks; let the soil dry completely between waterings.

SOIL • Well-draining potting mix amended with sand or orchid bark for added drainage.

FERTILIZER • In the growing season (spring to fall), feed with a balanced liquid fertilizer once a month at half the manufacturer's recommended rate. When plant growth slows in winter, stop fertilizing.

PESTS & DISEASE • While snake plants are generally pest resistant, they're somewhat susceptible to scale.

SHOPPING • Buy these slow growers at the size you want for display. Snake plants will become denser more quickly than they put on height; very large plants can be many years old.

POTTING • No need to stress about annual repotting as the plant grows— sansevierias prefer to be pot-bound.

PROPAGATION • Sansevierias have rhizomes that produce offsets, which can be separated from the mother plant and repotted. They can also be propagated with partial leaf cuttings.

Sansevieria

SNAKE PLANT

A LOW-MAINTENANCE STALWART that can be found in nearly every garden center, the snake plant is a great confidence booster for beginners. Native to dry and rocky habitats in western Africa, this plant can withstand challenging conditions indoors while offering a surprisingly splashy appearance.

When it comes to light and watering, a sansevieria is the perfect "get it and forget it" pick. While more light will increase its growth rate, this easygoing plant can survive in even the dimmest corner of the home. That makes it ideal for low-light spaces where most other plants will fail. Sansevierias prefer low humidity and can go weeks without watering. Their only request? Don't leave them in standing water.

While there are lots of practical reasons to choose a sansevieria, this grouping also offers a wide range of design options. From low-growing rosettes to tall cylinders and paddle-like stalks, there's a variety for every aesthetic. We're drawn to those with subtle coloration, preferring textural patterning to high-contrast yellow-and-green striped cultivars. *Sansevieria masoniana* 'Whale Fin' (pictured here) is quickly gaining popularity; its newly available variegated forms are particularly coveted. We also love the linear patterning of 'Sayuri', the mottled green hue of 'Jaboa', the silvery brightness of 'Moonshine', and the upright sharpness of 'Javelin'. Turn to pages 126–127 to see these varieties (and more!).

Trichilia emetica

NATAL MAHOGANY

IF YOU LOVE THE SCALE AND PRESENCE of indoor trees but feel intimidated by their reputation for fussiness, this evergreen native of southern Africa may be your perfect houseplant. Natal mahogany makes its home near rivers as an understory tree in tropical forests, so it's uniquely tolerant of both limited light and overwatering. For helicopter plant parents or those who want a large tree to anchor a darker space, this substantially sized species is the answer.

Because its native habitat offers predominantly dappled sunlight, Natal mahogany easily thrives in low, indirect light conditions that would challenge other leafy trees. It can even adjust to fluorescent lighting, so it's an excellent option for offices. Its riparian heritage confers another noteworthy quality: it can handle wet roots, and it won't struggle when overwatered like most trees. If you tend to fuss too much over your plants, Natal mahogany will bask in the extra attention.

This tropical tree pairs practical appeal with ample aesthetic charm. You'll most often find it planted as a cluster of five to ten saplings in a single pot, each one topped with glossy green leaves that produce an arching, graceful silhouette. When provided with a moderate amount of indirect light, it grows more rapidly than most comparable indoor trees. (It will reach an impactful height quickly but can easily be pruned to fit its location.) This makes Natal mahogany an excellent anchor plant for dim spaces, offering a lush and leafy look that brings the forest home.

LIGHT • Low to moderate indirect light. Can tolerate bright indirect light; avoid full sun.

WATER • Keep soil consistently moist but not soggy. Weekly watering is usually sufficient; don't let the soil dry out completely.

HUMIDITY • Benefits from humidity.

SOIL • Rich potting mix with good water retention.

FERTILIZER • Apply a slow-release granular indoor fertilizer every four to six months. Follow the manufacturer's instructions for rates and application. If the plant shows acute nutrient distress (leaf drop and discoloration) between granular feedings, sparingly apply a balanced liquid fertilizer every three or four waterings until distress abates.

PESTS & DISEASE • Scale can be an issue; due to dark stems, it's tough to spot the tiny, hard bumps until an infestation is advanced. Check plants carefully before buying. Also susceptible to spider mites.

SHOPPING • Natal mahogany is tougher to find, so buy whatever size you see! It's usually sold in a 10-inch (25 cm) pot. Specimens in that size pot will be about 3 to 5 feet (0.9 to 1.5 m) tall, the perfect floor-plant scale.

Zamioculcas zamiifolia 'Dowon'

ZZ RAVEN

BETTER KNOWN BY ITS INITIALS, *Zamioculcas zamiifolia* is a tough-as-nails member of an incredibly popular houseplant family: aroids. You'll find its trendy cousins in chapter one, but we've included the ZZ here because it handles challenging indoor conditions with grace. These plants are a time-tested staple for beginners, but new cultivars with designer appeal have caught the attention of experienced gardeners, too.

If you've grown a ZZ plant before, it was likely the ubiquitous green species. For a fresher option with the same low-key personality, look for the new 'Dowon' cultivar sold under the trade name Raven. Though its availability is inconsistent, Raven is exceptional; its new growth undergoes a transformation from bright green to nearly true black, a hue that's rare among indoor plants—and one that suits this plant's affinity for shadowy spaces.

Outstandingly durable, a ZZ plant is a reliable choice for your first-foray indoor plant or a space you've identified as a houseplant killer. Native to dry grasslands and forests in eastern Africa, the ZZ plant has a feature that allows it to withstand drought: It grows by means of rhizomes, underground stems that help it store water in addition to producing new roots and shoots. It can also handle sustained periods of low indirect light for much longer than other plants. A ZZ plant won't outgrow its pot too quickly, tolerates being pot-bound (like most rhizomatous plants), and excels as a low-maintenance mass planting—features that make it popular among both designers and home growers.

ZZ plants grow in an upright clump, with the largest specimens reaching about 4 feet (1.2 m) in both height and width. Ideal light and water conditions produce more rapid growth; in average conditions, the plant puts out new foliage at a moderate pace. Its upright habit makes the ZZ plant a great midsize floor plant. You can use it to enliven a dim corner, a room that receives limited light overall, or an entryway, since it's also tolerant of drafts.

LIGHT • Low indirect light is sufficient. Can tolerate bright indirect light; avoid full sun.

WATER • Water only when the soil is completely dry.

SOIL • Well-draining potting mix amended with sand or orchid bark for added drainage.

FERTILIZER • In the growing season (spring to fall), feed with a balanced liquid fertilizer once a month at half the manufacturer's recommended rate. When plant growth slows in winter, stop fertilizing.

PESTS & DISEASE • ZZ plants are somewhat susceptible to scale, mealybugs, and spider mites.

SHOPPING • Once very difficult to find, Raven is now consistently available. Growth is steady but not too rapid, so buy a size that suits your space.

POTTING • Wait until your plant is fully pot-bound before repotting. Extra soil can hold too much moisture, so keep the pot at a scale close to that of the root-ball.

FORM AND FUNCTION

Because these "unfussy friends" are so adaptable, they create opportunities for experimentation and are good candidates for placement in locations that are challenging for other houseplants. Case in point: these snake plants, filling the fireplace of a two-hundred-year-old farmhouse. This grouping addresses two decorative concerns at once: what to do with an empty fireplace during the off-season, and how to add greenery in a space with very limited light. At the same time, it creates a study in contrast between the spiky, modern plants and the formal shapes of a historic building.

While their function in the space is surprising, the sansevierias themselves are rich in interest, too; these practical plants often have more drama and style than we give them credit for. We started with a tonal palette of green, black, and silver to create this moody display, choosing varieties that offer subtle plays on leaf spotting and variegation (from left to right: *Sansevieria* 'Javelin', 'Jaboa', 'Sayuri', 'Javelin', 'Moonshine', 'Whale Fin', 'Moonshine', and 'Bantel's Sensation'). A mix of leaf sizes and textures adds variety, while simple modern pots create repetition to help the eye move smoothly throughout the collection.

FIVE

A CURIOUS CONSERVATORY

THE EVOCATIVE & ECLECTIC

WORLD OF FERNS

THERE'S SOMETHING UTTERLY CAPTIVATING ABOUT FERNS, their fronds curled like fingers that beckon us closer to reveal the intricacies of a single leaflet, a playfully ruffled edge, or a mysterious dusting of spores. Simultaneously dense and delicate, their foliage transports us to hushed woodland grottoes and dense tropical forests.

Among houseplant enthusiasts, ferns have a reputation for being fussy and intimidating, likely to die at the slightest hint of neglect. After tossing your fourth failed maidenhair into the trash, you might believe that reputation is well earned. While it's true that ferns are more sensitive than many other houseplants, if you understand their care requirements (regimented watering and lots of humidity) and find a species that matches your capacity for maintenance, they can be singularly rewarding companions.

Ferns encourage you to observe your surroundings frequently and thoughtfully, pausing for a moment to pick up your mister or simply admire the plants' lacy foliage. It's a joy to watch their fiddleheads reaching upward and gracefully unfurling to reveal new fronds. And unlike most houseplants, they continue to grow year-round, revealing new sensory pleasures throughout the seasons. Ferns may not be the best choice for true beginners, but they provide plant lovers with the chance to grow their abilities.

Davallia fejeensis 'Plumosa'

LACY RABBIT'S FOOT FERN

LIGHT • Bright indirect light.

WATER • Keep soil consistently moist during periods of active growth and let dry slightly between waterings outside the growing season. Don't water directly onto the rhizomes; aim for the surrounding soil. Avoid overwatering or waterlogged soil.

HUMIDITY • Benefits from humidity.

SOIL • Fluffy, finely textured, nutrient-rich potting mix.

FERTILIZER • In the growing season (spring to fall), feed sparingly with a balanced liquid fertilizer every two weeks at half the manufacturer's recommended rate. Your plant may rest in winter, but if it is still growing, fertilize once a month.

PESTS & DISEASE • Can be susceptible to scale.

SHOPPING • While standard rabbit's foot ferns are widely available, you're most likely to see 'Plumosa' offered by local specialty growers who are propagating it from older plants in their collections. It's fairly slow growing, so buy close to your desired size.

A RELATIVELY EASYGOING OPTION, *Davallia fejeensis* 'Plumosa' is a fantastic entry into the world of ferns. As its common name suggests, this cultivar is a lacier, old-fashioned iteration of the standard rabbit's foot fern, combining delicate foliage with a substantial scale, an open growth habit, and some delightful details. Each of its finely cut, triangular fronds can reach up to 20 inches (51 cm) long, creating a resplendent display of foliage.

Those fronds sprout from this fern's most intriguing feature: its rhizomes, a network of modified stems that form a network atop the surface of the soil. As shown at left, the golden brown and furry rhizomes of *D. fejeensis* resemble tiny paws, inspiring the species' common name. (Ferns that grow from rhizomes are collectively known as "footed ferns," and the rhizomes themselves vary widely; see E.T. fern on page 134 for an entirely different look.) Fronds emerge all along the rhizomes, so greenery spills in every direction as the network expands, creating multiple planes of growth for a lush, complex appearance.

This epiphytic fern is native to the islands of Fiji, where it clings to trees or rocks with those fuzzy rhizomes, collecting nutrients from air and water rather than soil. Because it doesn't require constant moisture, *D. fejeensis* is easier to care for than many ferns, offering the daintiness of a maidenhair (page 141) along with the ability to tolerate an occasional missed watering.

When displaying this fern, choose a vessel with enough soil surface area for its rhizomes to expand. Creeping outward, its fuzzy feet will eventually peep over the edge of the pot, adding a playful touch of contrasting texture below the lacy fronds.

Asplenium

BIRD'S-NEST FERN

BIRD'S-NEST FERNS HAVE BEEN A FAVORITE houseplant since Victorian times, when a fern craze known as pteridomania swept the plant world and catapulted them to popularity. More than a century later, we still love this broad subgroup for its regal form and relatively undemanding nature.

Bird's-nest ferns differ from the other genuses in this chapter because their fronds grow from one central point, gradually peeling back to create a dignified silhouette that can reach 5 feet (1.5 m) tall and 3 feet (0.9 m) wide. Many plants with this sort of height develop wildly irregular forms, but most bird's-nest varieties maintain predictable shapes. Though native to the warm, humid rain forests of the Pacific Basin, they're hardier as houseplants than other classic ferns, making them a fantastic low-maintenance, high-impact piece for the home.

Aspleniums are well established in the houseplant world, but new cultivars are enlivening the genus. For a classical look, consider 'Victoria' bird's-nest fern (*Asplenium antiquum* 'Victoria'), a vintage variety with ruffled leaves. A relatively new variety, pictured here, *A. antiquum* 'Hurricane' offers an atypical look: wavy, sometimes forked fronds that grow in a tidy and persistent spiral pattern (see page 155 for a view of the pattern from overhead). Another new favorite is Champion bird's-nest fern (*A. nidus* 'Campio'), which has lightly dissected fronds that vary significantly from one to the next, a novel touch of randomness in a genus known for regularity. And check out the heavily ruffled frond of *A. musifolium plicata* 'Cobra' pictured on page 154.

A small-scale bird's-nest fern like 'Hurricane' will excel as a tabletop plant or in a mixed grouping where it can serve as the understory below more high-branching neighbors. We prefer to display larger varieties like *A. nidus* as single specimens with underplantings, filling a corner with greenery or perched up high to better show off their regal forms.

LIGHT • Bright indirect light. Bird's-nest ferns are light sensitive and can't tolerate direct sun.

WATER • Maintain moist, but not wet, soil. These ferns are susceptible to rot or damage at their centers, so water from below by placing the plant into a tray of water and letting the soil wick water upward for at least an hour.

HUMIDITY • Benefits from humidity.

SOIL • Fluffy, finely textured, nutrient-rich potting mix.

FERTILIZER • In the growing season (spring to fall), feed with a balanced liquid fertilizer every two weeks at half the manufacturer's recommended rate. Your plant may rest in winter, but if it is still growing, fertilize once a month.

SHOPPING • Bird's-nest ferns are slow growing and can be found at any size, from tiny 2-inch (5 cm) plants to enormous, 5-foot (1.5 m) tall specimens.

Polypodium formosanum 'Cristatum'

E.T. FERN

THE E.T. FERN is a relative newcomer to the houseplant world. It emerged over the last five years and has quickly become one of our favorites for its caterpillar-like network of rhizomes that grows laterally atop the surface of the soil. Nubby, electric green, and succulent-like, these "feet" have an alien appearance that calls to mind the fingers of a famous on-screen extraterrestrial.

Soaring above this dense and texturally complex foundation, the E.T. fern's crown of foliage creates multiple levels of interest. Its heavily dissected fronds are accented by dark veining that extends from the center down the length of each leaflet. The fronds sprout compact and upright from the rhizomes but lengthen to develop a draping silhouette as they mature. Along with this charmingly quirky appearance, the E.T. fern boasts an easygoing nature; it's more resilient than many fern varieties.

E.T. ferns are native to East Asia, where they primarily grow as epiphytes, clinging to tree trunks and rocks. As houseplants, they are equally content to grow in pots. For this species and all footed ferns, consider a planter with a flared silhouette. Its wide top will allow extra surface area to showcase the rhizomes' ambling growth. The rhizome network spreads to cover any available soil surface area as the plant becomes more established, creating a fascinating labyrinthine display. As its dense fronds and outlandish rhizomes develop, the E.T. fern's otherworldly appearance will make it a welcome addition to your home.

LIGHT • While it grows best in bright indirect light, the E.T. fern—unlike many ferns—will maintain a healthy appearance when a window or light source is slightly more distant.

WATER • Water thoroughly every three or four days, pouring in water until it drains through the soil into the saucer. Wait thirty minutes, then drain any excess water. Crispy edges will develop if the plant gets too dry; in many cases, you can trim those edges or fronds and the plant will recover.

HUMIDITY • Benefits from humidity.

SOIL • Fluffy, finely textured, nutrient-rich potting mix.

FERTILIZER • In the growing season (spring to fall), feed with a balanced liquid fertilizer every two weeks at half the manufacturer's recommended rate. Your plant may rest in winter, but if it is still growing, fertilize once a month.

Psilotum nudum

SKELETON FORK FERN

THE SCIENTIFIC NAME *PSILOTUM NUDUM* comes from the Latin for "bare naked," an apt description for what is undoubtedly one of the strangest members of the fern family. This outlier is actually a primitive predecessor to ferns; it shares many characteristics and anatomic structures with its leafy compatriots but bears little resemblance to more familiar varieties. Also known as the "whisk fern," it's closer in appearance to a succulent or cactus. The skeleton fork fern is made up of slender leafless stems, sparsely adorned with bulbous, spore-producing growths at the tips. A good option for those who are bad with ferns, it offers a fern silhouette stripped down to suit a minimalist aesthetic, with care requirements to match.

Unique in that they lack both leaves and roots, plants in the genus *Psilotum* are sometimes called living fossils. Native to a wide range of tropical and subtropical regions, they grow from rhizomes instead of roots and can be epiphytic, meaning they can grow without soil, deriving the moisture and nutrients they need from air and water. In the wild, epiphytes can be found atop rocks or on the surface of another plant, but as a houseplant, *P. nudum* is generally sold as a potted specimen—and that's fine, because it's adaptable and sturdy (it also requires less water than most ferns, since it doesn't have leaves to feed).

This atypical plant is by no means petite, reaching up to 18 inches (45 cm) wide, but its willowy habit takes up less visual space than that of its foliage-heavy counterparts. It's an outstanding addition to mixed plantings, where its spare silhouette provides textural contrast for lush-foliage plants like the E.T. fern (page 134) and aroids (see chapter one). We like it most, however, as a single "pet" specimen, which allows its curious details to shine. It is precisely those details that stopped us in our tracks when we first spotted it growing from a wall in the fern garden at Chicago's Garfield Park Conservatory (see page 247).

LIGHT • Bright indirect light.

WATER • Allow the soil to lightly dry between waterings, then water thoroughly.

HUMIDITY • Benefits from humidity.

SOIL • Fluffy, finely textured, nutrient-rich potting mix.

FERTILIZER • In the growing season (spring to fall), feed sparingly with a balanced liquid fertilizer once a month at half the manufacturer's recommended rate. When plant growth slows in winter, stop fertilizing.

PESTS & DISEASE • Most ferns are fairly pest resistant, but this variety can be susceptible to mealybugs.

SHOPPING • These strange specimens are relatively rare and available only through specialty growers. If you find one, buy it!

GROWTH • Skeleton fork ferns are slow growers; don't expect drastic changes in size or the frequent appearance of unfurling shoots and fronds common to other species.

Asparagus setaceus

ASPARAGUS PLUMOSA FERN

THE COMMON NAME "ASPARAGUS FERN" applies to a wide variety of plants, but it most often refers to *Asparagus setaceus* (formerly *A. plumosus*). These natives of coastal South Africa enjoyed a surge of popularity during the houseplant heyday of the 1970s. Enchanted by their ambling silhouette and intricate texture, we believe they're overdue for a revival.

The asparagus fern's common name is somewhat misleading because it's not a fern at all—it's a member of the asparagus family. We've grouped it with true ferns, however, because its feather-like fronds invite similar design applications. Those "fronds" are technically cladophylls: flattened branches that function as leaves. The branches have a fine, needlelike texture and, unlike those of true ferns, grow in plateaus instead of the more typical arches, creating a dense thicket with both vertical and horizontal interest. Mature asparagus ferns can reach 2 feet (0.6 m) tall with cladophylls up to 6 feet (1.8 m) long. This expansive display of foliage sprouts from a central clump above tuberous roots that are used to store moisture. The roots can reach incredible sizes, sometimes breaking through their pots!

Asparagus ferns have a delicacy that allows them to serve as "punctuation mark" plants, instantly enlivening indoor spaces. Their fine-filigree texture provides a counterpoint to the current trend of "home jungles" by breaking up collections of broad-leaved tropicals. We also love these graceful specimens when displayed in multiples; see an example on pages 148–149.

LIGHT • Bright indirect light. Full sun will cause foliage to become bleached or discolored.

WATER • Water thoroughly every three or four days, pouring in water until it drains through the soil into the saucer. Wait thirty minutes, then drain any excess water. Though delicate in appearance, these ferns are hardier than most. They'll tolerate some dryness, though too little water can cause browning and leaf drop.

HUMIDITY • Benefits from humidity.

SOIL • Fluffy, finely textured, nutrient-rich potting mix.

FERTILIZER • In the growing season (spring to fall), feed sparingly with a balanced liquid fertilizer once a month at half the manufacturer's recommended rate. When plant growth slows in winter, stop fertilizing.

PESTS & DISEASE • Asparagus ferns are susceptible to mealybugs.

POTTING • Because of their large roots, these ferns get pot-bound quickly. They'll continue to grow if repotted in increasingly larger vessels.

HANDLING • Handle with care when moving or repotting—many varieties have thorny stems!

Adiantum

MAIDENHAIR FERN

YOU'VE LIKELY SPOTTED cloudlike maidenhair ferns gracing public spaces like hotel lobbies or cascading down the vertical surface of an office's green wall. These popular houseplants are the most delicate and beautiful member of the fern family, with an airy anatomy that has entranced generations of plant lovers. Feathery fronds of tiny, nearly translucent leaves suspended from wire-thin stems give maidenhairs an irresistibly tactile appeal.

Elevated but not excessively ornate, these ferns are remarkably versatile. They work well in woodland-inspired container plantings, surrounded with moss and twigs to mimic their native habitat on the forest floor. We also love using them in multiples (as seen on pages 148–149); a large swath of their finely textured foliage is particularly pleasing.

Maidenhairs have a reputation for being demanding, but as long as you maintain a disciplined watering schedule, they are incredibly hardy. They do appreciate humidity, so consider placing them in a kitchen or bath (which naturally has higher ambient humidity than elsewhere in the home), or pairing them with a humidity tray—see page 27, where one is shown with an *Adiantum fragrans*. Meet these needs and they'll reward you with a beautiful growth process; new fronds unfurl elegantly from their centers, inviting a closer look whenever you pass by.

A. microphyllum 'Little Lady' is pictured at right; turn the page for more on this and three of our other favorite varieties of maidenhair.

LIGHT • Very bright indirect light. Can tolerate very early morning sun but will burn in full sun.

WATER • Water thoroughly every two or three days, pouring in water until it fills a large saucer. Let the plant rest in the saucer for thirty minutes, then empty the saucer or move the plant to a humidity tray. Fronds will curl or crinkle if the plant becomes too dry. Water immediately if you see these signs, but fair warning: it may be too late.

HUMIDITY • Benefits from humidity.

SOIL • Fluffy, finely textured, nutrient-rich potting mix.

FERTILIZER • In the growing season (spring to fall), feed with a balanced liquid fertilizer every two weeks at half the manufacturer's recommended rate. Your plant may rest in winter, but if it is still growing, fertilize once a month.

SHOPPING • Buy for the space you have in mind. The largest specimens reach about 24 inches (61 cm) tall and require a 10-inch (25 cm) pot. If you're nervous about watering, choose a more established plant, which will have more soil and thus dry out more slowly.

POTTING • A pot with a finish or glaze will help water evaporate more slowly— but it should have a drainage hole. Repot yearly.

MAIDENHAIR FERN

Adiantum microphyllum
'Little Lady'

Incredibly fine, this miniature maidenhair is topped with a multitude of leaflets, each one the size of a pencil tip. This fern's frothy foliage takes the iconic maidenhair texture to an extraordinarily delicate place, while its diminutive size makes it a sweet companion on your desk or windowsill. It's also slightly more tolerant of a delay in watering than a classic maidenhair.

Adiantum raddianum
'Pacific Maid'

This compact variety features densely bunched leaves on shrubby stems, which create a ruffled effect. We love the contrast born of planting it alongside more feathery ferns like 'Little Lady'.

Adiantum peruvianum
Silver dollar fern

A spreading architectural habit and large disklike leaves with pointed tips give this species a more substantial presence than other maidenhairs. As the plant grows, the leaf-laden fronds develop a graceful, downward-arching silhouette. New growth emerges dusty pink, maturing to solid green. Slightly more tolerant of underwatering than some other maidenhairs, silver dollar ferns can be a good introduction to the category. Don't stress if you see browning at the leaf tips—this fern develops well-defined spores that give this effect.

Adiantum hispidulum
'Bronze Venus'

This uniquely colorful variety features palmate fronds that emerge in a beguiling shade of bronze-red and mature to dark green. We love its graceful, arching habit and the open profile created by its shapely fronds.

Polypodium aureum 'Mandaianum'

CRESTED BEAR'S PAW FERN

THE SHOWIEST STATEMENT PIECE in our fern collection, crested bear's paw fern can reach 3½ feet (1.1 m) in height with single fronds more than 3 feet (0.9 m) long. This structural species is somewhat difficult to find but well worth the hunt for those seeking a dramatic combination of color, texture, and size—plus a few unexpected details.

At first glance, you'll notice two things about the crested bear's paw fern: a chalky, glaucous blue hue and a profusion of highly textural fronds. The fronds develop densely ruffled edges as they mature, giving this substantial plant a lacy feel. The species gets its name from the "cresting" that occurs at the tips of mature fronds: each one forks into multiple points, adding to the plant's ruffled appearance. The fronds reach skyward and outward, creating an upright yet spreading habit that makes this fern a grand presence at a younger age than most varieties.

While many ferns are best as tabletop specimens, crested bear's paw fern has the scale to be a floor plant, perfect for areas that need a bold infusion of greenery. Native to subtropical and tropical regions of the Americas, it grows in the wild as an understory plant; this means it can survive in rooms that offer only indirect light, if placed near a window. It also produces fantastic fiddleheads and big, woolly rhizomes that creep across the surface of the soil as it grows. These intriguing details reward the observer who takes a step closer, admiring this fern's intricacy as well as its remarkable size.

LIGHT • Bright indirect light. More tolerant to low-light conditions than many ferns.

WATER • Water thoroughly every two or three days, pouring in water until it drains through the soil into the saucer. Wait thirty minutes, then drain any excess water. Water only from the side of the pot; watering in the center where the leaves emerge may cause leaf drop.

HUMIDITY • Provide lots of humidity and mist regularly.

SOIL • Fluffy, finely textured, nutrient-rich potting mix.

FERTILIZER • In the growing season (spring to fall), feed with a balanced liquid fertilizer every two weeks at half the manufacturer's recommended rate. Your plant may rest in winter, but if it is still growing, fertilize once a month.

SHOPPING • These ferns take a while to reach maturity, so to immediately enjoy one's size and impact, buy an 8-inch (20 cm) pot or larger.

Pyrrosia lingua 'Variegata'

VARIEGATED TONGUE FERN

ONE OF OUR FAVORITE THINGS about ferns is their incredible diversity in texture, ranging from the featherlight foliage of the maidenhair (page 141) to the curiously bare silhouette of the skeleton fork (page 137) to the shapely fronds of the tongue fern. Understated and elegant, we love the variegated cultivar of this fern for both its foliage and its form.

Pyrrosia lingua has stiffer, thicker fronds than most ferns, each one supported by a wiry stem. The rippled fronds reach up to 18 inches (46 cm) tall at maturity and can be solid bright green or variegated (as shown here). They also possess a fuzzy allover texture—denser on their undersides than their tops—that creates a soft, matte appearance. Some fronds will fork at the tips as they grow (a process known as cresting), adding intricacy to the plant's silhouette.

Below these eye-catching fronds, you'll find another intriguing feature: small, woody, and wonderfully irregular rhizomes. Fronds can sprout at any point on a rhizome, giving the fern a progressively bushier silhouette as it produces new foliage.

Tongue ferns grow as understory epiphytes in their native Southeast Asia, anchoring themselves to rocks and trees with their rhizomes. As houseplants, however, they're usually potted. You may find them to be slower growing and fussier than many other specimens in your collection, but your patience and diligent care will be rewarded as these fascinating ferns mature, proud new fronds unfurling while ever-curious rhizomes roam below.

LIGHT • Bright indirect light. Can tolerate morning sun.

WATER • Water when the top inch (2.5 cm) of soil becomes dry. Don't water directly onto the rhizomes; aim for the surrounding soil. Because it's an epiphyte, this fern can't tolerate soggy soil, so avoid overwatering. If too dry, the leaves will start to shrivel, but the plant can recover if you resume a regular watering routine.

HUMIDITY • Benefits from humidity.

SOIL • Fluffy, finely textured, nutrient-rich potting mix.

FERTILIZER • In the growing season (spring to fall), feed with a balanced liquid fertilizer once a month at half the manufacturer's recommended rate. When plant growth slows in winter, stop fertilizing.

PESTS & DISEASE • Scale can be an issue due to this fern's woody stems and rhizomes.

SHOPPING • Buy this less-common fern when you see it; availability is intermittent. Because it grows slowly, you'll usually find it in 4- to 6-inch (10 to 15 cm) pots.

POTTING • Rhizomes are shallow but need room to expand outward; they will grow to the space provided. Pot in a container with some extra soil surface area and up-pot when the rhizomes need additional space. Increase pot sizes gradually for these slow growers.

MANY MAKE ONE

Ferns are a broad group in terms of scale and texture, which allows for a wealth of design options.
While many varieties have the gravitas to stand
alone, ferns are most impactful when used to create maxed-out displays. Asparagus and maidenhair
ferns, as seen here, are our favorite options for
curating this look. Together they create a singularly lush effect that's rich in textural contrast,
the maidenhairs serving as a dense yet delicate
counterpoint to the profuse asparagus ferns.

To unify many plants in a grouping, consider
a tonal palette when choosing your containers.
Here, pale Italian terra-cotta pots paired with
beige and white vessels provide a consistent, neutral base for the abundant greenery.

CENTRAL FLORIDA FERNS & FOLIAGE

ZELLWOOD, FLORIDA

For over thirty years, three generations of the Roberts family have cultivated a spectacular assortment of ferns and leafy houseplants at Central Florida Ferns & Foliage. As CFF enters its fourth decade, second-generation operator Matt Roberts looks back on his father Ray's early days in the business—and forward to their evolving industry.

"Plants were always a hobby for my dad," says Matt. "Even in high school, he helped build and repair greenhouses." Another high school job—growing leatherleaf ferns for florists—was an early indicator that these plants would become Ray's passion. He eventually started working part-time at a nursery called Vincent's, which specialized in exotic tropical ferns. After eleven years as a firefighter and paramedic, Ray went full-time at Vincent's; when the owner retired in 1990, Ray took over his phone and fax numbers, and with them, his customer base. "At the time, having a fax number was a huge deal!" says Matt. Fax number in hand, CFF was born.

Exotic ferns had long been Ray's favorite plants; as his business expanded, so did his personal collection of rare species, sourced from friends and fellow enthusiasts. "He was swapping plants before it was cool," Matt says with a laugh. Ray filled a collection house with tree ferns, staghorns, and selaginellas; most have now been donated to local botanical gardens. "Sometimes we kick ourselves for giving them away, but it's great to see that legacy carried on." Matt pauses, adding, "We're thinking of starting a collection house again."

"We" at CFF now includes Ray and his wife, Kathy; Matt; and Ray and Kathy's grandson Logan

Boston ferns suspended above rows of ficuses reflect CFF's expansion into categories beyond ferns. As the business grows, they're adding solar panels and reducing water waste in newer greenhouses, like this one. "Lots of people think that growers are polluters, but we're environmentally minded. We're good stewards of the land," says Matt.

VanderMaas. Matt, who has been in the greenhouse for as long as he can remember, joined full-time in 2010. "After college, I came to work here for what was supposed to be six months. I fell in love with plants and wanted to continue our legacy. Now I'm rooted in." He handles sales and marketing; Logan, passionate about growing plants, is following in his grandfather's footsteps.

CFF started with 25,000 square feet (2,300 sq m) of greenhouse space; today, its four locations account for nearly 400,000 square feet (37,000 sq m). Ray has always envisioned the business as a one-stop shop that offers "a little bit of a lot," brokering plants from other nurseries alongside his own. (One of CFF's first partners was Harmony—see page 104—whose begonia specialists named a hybrid 'Harmony's Ray Glo' in his honor.) "Variety is our biggest strength and

our biggest challenge," Matt explains. "We thrive in controlled chaos, but mixing plants in the greenhouse presents watering and pest challenges. Expanding lets us keep plants with separate needs separate and do things more efficiently."

Among all the plants in CFF's greenhouses, maidenhair ferns are Matt's favorites. "Maidenhairs are tough for many growers, but they're so beautiful when you get them right. I take pride in offering a wide range of sizes and varieties." The key to success? Keeping moisture and humidity tailored to these fussy ferns' needs—a difficult task in the local

ABOVE: From left to right: Logan, Matt, Ray, and Kyle, a longtime employee at CFF. OPPOSITE, CLOCKWISE FROM TOP LEFT: A crocodile fern (*Microsorum musifolium*); a mix of *Pteris* fern varieties; one of CFF's older greenhouses that provides space for shade-loving ferns (see a newer-style greenhouse on page 151).

climate. Nearby Apopka is the "indoor foliage capital of the world," but ferns aren't often grown in Florida because excessive heat slows their growth. CFF uses wet-pad cooling systems during the summer months; in winter, the warm climate is beneficial, extending the growing season and limiting the need for heating. Matt says, "There's something addictive about the challenges of maidenhairs—if you kill one, you buy two more!"

And today, there are lots of buyers. "Plants are probably as popular as they've ever been," Matt reflects. "Old-school growers compare the current trend to the popularity of houseplants in the 1970s, but there's a big difference: people were starting greenhouses then. Nobody is now." As land prices rise, older nursery owners are selling their property and retiring. When specialty growers shutter, their legacy and knowledge are lost. As a board member of the Florida Nursery, Growers & Landscape Association, Matt wants to change that. "The hardest part is helping younger people realize they want to be in this industry. It's a lot of hard work, but there are a lot of hard workers! FNGLA is our statewide voice, so we're creating an apprenticeship program to find people who can thrive here."

Along with the search for new people, there's the constant search for new plants. "We offer practically every fern available, but there's room for more foliage—exotic new varieties and harder-to-find classics, too. Historically great houseplants like *Pilea mollis* 'Moon Valley' are getting popular again. It energizes us to see people excited about plants that we've always known are awesome. Now we get to bring them to new customers."

As a parting thought, Matt shared a recent conversation with a fellow grower: "He said, 'Now everything you want is right on your phone. Plants are the complete opposite.' They teach patience, time, attention to detail." Plants invite us to slow down in a frenetic world. They help us appreciate growth and change across time—across the Roberts family's generations, and for generations to come.

ABOVE: The ruffled fronds of *Asplenium musifolium plicata* 'Cobra'. RIGHT: As CFF broadens their offering beyond ferns, they're following the market into new trendy plants like anthurium. Seen here, the high-contrast *Anthurium crystallinum*. OPPOSITE: The beguiling swirl of a 'Hurricane' bird's-nest fern.

SIX

LIVING SCULPTURES

SUN-LOVING SUCCULENTS & CACTI

SUCCULENTS AND CACTI ARE LIKE GOOD ROOMMATES: they're low maintenance, get along well with others, and just need a sunny corner to be content. For novices or those who prefer a "get it and forget it" approach to houseplants, these easygoing specimens are a perfect match.

While their undemanding nature is a plus for beginners and busy green thumbs, there's much more to love about succulents and cacti. Both architectural and textural, they offer a breadth of shapes, colors, patterns, and sizes that invites adventurous and playful design applications. Their otherworldly appearances bring home a novel taste of arid and unfamiliar landscapes, particularly for those who don't live near desert climes.

The word "succulent" may call to mind compact, tidy rosettes of fleshy leaves, but this group is far more diverse and often quite sculptural. Many, including graptopetalum (page 158) and astrophytum (page 168), excel at pattern repetition with pleasingly geometric growth. Other succulents and cacti develop wilder structures; consider the spiky drama of aloe, graphic paddles of opuntia, or upright grace of euphorbia. Myriad textures and colors appear within each silhouette—prickly to plush, glaucous blue to fiery red—offering greater variety than nearly any other category of houseplants.

GRAPTOPETALUM

LIGHT • Full sun. At least six hours of direct light daily.

WATER • Choose a container with ample drainage, and water only when the soil is completely dry. Reduce watering in winter. Wrinkled leaves indicate underwatering.

SOIL • Well-draining, coarse succulent mix.

FERTILIZER • Feed sparingly with a low-nitrogen liquid fertilizer once a month at half the manufacturer's recommended rate or less. Graptopetalum plants need lots of light if being fed; plants in low-light conditions should receive even less supplemental fertility. Do not feed in winter.

HANDLING • Avoid moving or repotting graptopetalums as much as possible. They propagate from leaves or rosettes that fall off, a natural adaptation that makes them fragile. It's better to allow your plant to become pot-bound than to repot it.

PRUNING • Graptopetalums produce new growth from the center of each rosette. To keep a compact shape, pinch back any stems that become too rangy.

PROPAGATION • Can be propagated with succulent leaf cuttings. Leaves or rosettes that fall from the mother plant into the pot will often root on their own.

GRAPTOPETALUM PARAGUAYENSE is perfect for those seeking a classic rosette-shaped succulent with a few extra flourishes. Combining a rangy silhouette with astonishing blooms, it's a statement plant with the low-maintenance needs of a succulent, preferring bright, dry conditions that mimic its native habitat in Mexico.

Above all else, we adore the graptopetalum for its flowers. Arcing floral bracts tower above the rosettes in a long-lasting display that changes throughout the growing season (which will vary based on your region's available light but generally begins in late winter—unfortunately too late for us to have captured it in these photos). These bracts emerge as fleshy stems matching the color and texture of the leaves, then explode into plumes of flowers suspended on wire-thin stems in early spring. As the blooms fade, their dried remains create a frothy, textural cloud, lingering over the plant for a month or more.

While those flowers are reason enough to head to the nursery, there's more to love about *G. paraguayense*. Unlike other rosette-forming succulents, graptopetalums have a rambling habit with rosettes that drip from long, cascading branches. Exposure to full sunlight brightens this species' leaves to shades of pink or purple, while partial shade produces cooler blue-gray hues. A dusty, pearlescent overtone inspires its common name: ghost plant.

Its delicate silhouette and extraordinary flowers make this succulent a stunning option to display as a single wild specimen. Consider placement in a tall urn or on a high shelf to make the most of the trailing habit. We also love graptopetalums planted en masse, so their blooms can form a dramatic cloud above the grouping. They're an asset for adding contrast in mixed plantings as well, offering an airiness rarely seen in the succulent world.

Kalanchoe gastonis-bonnieri

DONKEY EAR PLANT

GENUS *KALANCHOE* contains over 125 species; compact, flowering varieties are a garden center staple, but we favor specimens where the genus's spectacular range of foliage—replete with otherworldly shapes, unexpected textures, and bold colors—takes center stage. And when it comes to foliage, our favorite of the group is *K. gastonis-bonnieri*.

This fast-growing species, commonly called the donkey ear plant, stands out thanks to its serrated leaves, which emerge pale green and mature to a vivid lime hue. Each oversize leaf is banded with splashy tiger stripes and topped off by a glaucous coating for a frosty overall effect. Like many kalanchoes, *K. gastonis-bonnieri* will take on a reddish hue if exposed to cooler temperatures; try leaving it outside on cool nights when conditions won't drop below freezing.

The quirky appearance of this kalanchoe is matched by a peculiar growth cycle. A *K. gastonis-bonnieri* plant flowers only once, declining and dying after it blooms. You can extend its life span by pinching back any flower stalks that shoot up from its center, which will prevent blooms and keep it growing as usual. But if you'd like to let your plant bloom (the flowers are quite lovely!), it will provide its own replacement. *K. gastonis-bonnieri* produces plantlets, juvenile plants that sprout from the mother plant's leaf margins, most often at the tip of the leaf. These can be used to propagate new plants, so you can enjoy generation after generation of showy succulents.

With its vibrant foliage and profusion of plantlets, *K. gastonis-bonnieri* is well suited for display as a stand-alone specimen. Pot in a proportionately taller vessel, like an urn, or place on a plant stand to showcase its gently draping leaves and the tiny, dangling plantlets that serve as delightful natural ornaments.

LIGHT • Direct to bright indirect light; keep out of direct sun during the hottest parts of the day.

WATER • Choose a pot with ample drainage, and water only when the soil is completely dry. Reduce watering in winter. Wrinkled leaves indicate underwatering.

SOIL • Well-draining, coarse succulent mix.

FERTILIZER • Feed sparingly with a low-nitrogen liquid fertilizer once a month at half the manufacturer's recommended rate or less. Kalanchoes need lots of light if being fed; plants in low-light conditions should receive even less supplemental fertility. Do not feed in winter.

POTTING • Repot yearly.

HANDLING • Kalanchoes often have caustic sap that can cause skin irritation. Handle with care and keep out of reach of kids or pets.

PROPAGATION • *K. gastonis-bonnieri* propagates very easily from succulent leaf cuttings or via plantlets.

EUPHORBIA

WE LOVE EUPHORBIA for their fascinating diversity. Members of the genus range from hardy, leafy perennials (*Euphorbia* 'Blackbird') to a classic holiday bloom: the poinsettia (*E. pulcherrima*). Here, however, we've focused on upright cactus-like silhouettes such as *E. lactea* 'White Ghost' (pictured at left). Learn more about this and three of our other favorite specimens on pages 164–165. With undemanding care requirements and the ability to thrive indoors, these succulents have become popular houseplants for those seeking both architectural shapes and vibrant blooms.

Euphorbias vary so spectacularly in appearance because they're native to a range of climates across tropical Africa and Madagascar. In spite of their far-flung origins, these plants share a few traits. All species have a distinctive, latex-like white sap. (Note: This caustic sap can cause skin irritation or harm if ingested, so take care when handling your plant.) Perennial and flowering succulent varieties produce distinctive blooms with a cuplike silhouette. Many species also share an upright and prickly appearance, which can be misleading because euphorbias aren't cacti—the structure of their spines creates a subtle distinction (cactus spines are modified leaves, while euphorbia spines are thorns, meaning that euphorbias can have both leaves *and* thorns)—as seen opposite, where red leaves follow the thorns up *E. trigona rubrum*.

Upright specimens have a stately presence, perfect for framing large windows and doors in spaces with lots of natural light. They're also fantastic for adding scale to mixed containers, serving as a background story for a planting of low-growing succulents. Euphorbias offer the vertical impact of cacti with the range of patterns, shapes, and colors found in succulents—a true "best of both worlds" moment.

LIGHT • Four hours of direct light daily, or all-day indirect light.

WATER • Choose a container with ample drainage, and water only when the soil is completely dry. Reduce watering in winter. Wrinkled leaves indicate underwatering.

SOIL • Well-draining, coarse succulent mix.

FERTILIZER • Feed sparingly with a low-nitrogen liquid fertilizer once a month at half the manufacturer's recommended rate or less. Euphorbia plants need lots of light if being fed; plants in low-light conditions should receive even less supplemental fertility. Do not feed in winter.

SHOPPING • Like most succulents, euphorbia are slow growers indoors. Purchase a larger plant if you're looking for an impactful presence in your space.

POTTING • Repot yearly.

EUPHORBIA

Euphorbia ammak
'Variegata'

Commonly known as the "candelabra tree" for its upright, branching habit, this cultivar offers a quintessential desert silhouette. It's ideal for those seeking a graphic look; marbled variegations in creamy yellow and pale green lend its leaves a reptilian effect. Though slow growing indoors, it can reach a mature height of 15 to 20 feet (4.5 to 6 m).

Euphorbia lactea
'White Ghost'

For a similar high-contrast variegation to *E. ammak* but at a smaller scale, consider this curiously colored cultivar, which features a blanched central stem framed by spiny, dark green ribs. 'White Ghost' grows to about half the height of its larger cousin, making it an ideal choice for smaller spaces.

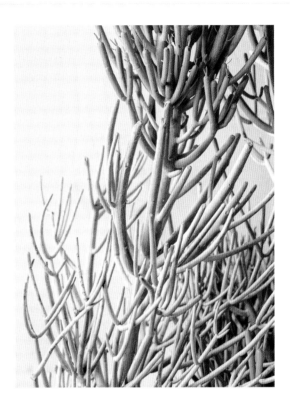

Euphorbia ingens

Candelabra tree

Another upright option, *E. ingens* shares its common name and distinctive shape with *E. ammak*. In place of *E. ammak*'s variegations, this species offers a consistent, saturated green hue, perfect for accenting spaces that are rich in pattern or texture or for punctuating large swaths of bold color.

Euphorbia tirucalli

Firesticks

Also known as "pencil cactus," this succulent shrub forms a thicket of narrow, upward-reaching branches, lending it a coral-like appearance. The branch tips can bleach in the sun or turn a vibrant red with exposure to cooler temperatures (but never expose it to frost!).

Opuntia

PRICKLY PEAR CACTUS

IN THE WIDE WORLD OF CACTI, the opuntia stands alone. We mean that literally, since genus *Opuntia* contains only one very famous member: the prickly pear cactus. This singularity, however, doesn't translate to a lack of variety; with over two hundred species of prickly pear, opuntias offer a scale and style for every home.

Prickly pears are widely distributed across Mexico, California, and the southwestern deserts of the United States. Their fleshy paddles, called cladodes, can take the form of narrow ovals, circular platters, or densely stacked clusters. The opuntia's atypical growth habit—one paddle sprouting from the next without a stem in between—lends it a graphic shape that's more feminine than that of traditional upright cacti. This iconic silhouette has also made opuntia a trendy inspiration for pattern work in textiles and printmaking.

While this stacked paddle structure is fairly consistent across all cultivars, opuntias diverge widely in scale, texture, and color. They come in a rainbow of hues, from dusty plum and glaucous blue to deep forest green peppered with golden dots. Some are studded with spines, while others, like the *Opuntia cacanapa* 'Ellisiana' (shown opposite), are entirely smooth. *O. microdasys* (aka bunny ears cactus; pictured at right), a fuzzy garden center staple with tiny 1-inch (2.5 cm) paddles, is a perfect introduction to the genus. Collectors seeking a showstopper should consider *O. santarita* (Santa Rita prickly pear), a towering species with foot-wide (30 cm) paddles in vivid purple, or *O. gomei* 'Old Mexico', equally large with an undulating form. This stunning diversity makes the world of opuntia a designer's wonderland—turn to pages 172–173 for our favorite way to showcase these specimens.

LIGHT • Bright direct light.

WATER • Choose a container with ample drainage, and water only when the soil is completely dry. Reduce watering in winter. Wrinkled leaves indicate underwatering.

SOIL • Well-draining, coarse succulent mix.

FERTILIZER • Feed sparingly with a low-nitrogen liquid fertilizer once a month at half the manufacturer's recommended rate or less. Prickly pears need lots of light if being fed; plants in low-light conditions should receive even less supplemental feeding. Do not feed in winter.

TEMPERATURE • Prickly pears require a consistent temperature; avoid exposure to drafts and heat sources.

POTTING • Repot yearly.

HANDLING • Handle with care: many prickly pears have spines, so wear sturdy gloves when potting or moving.

Astrophytum asterias

STAR CACTUS

THERE IS, PERHAPS, NO CACTUS MORE CHARMING than an astrophytum. These petite specimens have a visually pleasing star shape (the name *Astrophytum* comes from the Greek for "star" and "plant") formed by well-defined vertical ribs. This sharply ribbed silhouette also lends them another evocative common name: "bishop's hat cactus."

Thanks to their unconventional shape, sweetly petite stature, and vivid textural variations, star cacti have become an obsession for collectors, particularly in the Japanese and western US plant communities. Aficionados delight in trading exceptionally rare variegated cultivars. When searching for your own astrophytum, you may see plants with three to eight ribs; five is most common. As they age, the ribs develop white, sometimes woolly, spots or scales called areolas (or areoles), which can be scattered for a polka-dot appearance or arranged in geometric patterns for a tidy graphic effect. Though these cacti may sprout a single bloom at the top of the plant, they're prized for their eccentric forms more than for their flowers.

Native to the highlands of central and northern Mexico, these cacti thrive in dry, stony soil. They're good neighbors in mixed indoor rock gardens, since many don't have spines to injure other plants, but their small scale makes it easy to lose them in the shuffle of a mixed planting. We recommend giving them the spotlight as a single specimen, or grouping several together so they won't be overshadowed by larger plants. A planting of a few species with varied textures creates an enchanting jewel-box effect. No matter how you pot them, place them in a bright location where they'll be noticed—they're sure to spark a smile or a conversation from every passerby.

LIGHT • Six or more hours of indirect light daily. Ambient light from a south-facing window is ideal. Protect from direct sun.

WATER • Choose a container with ample drainage, and water only when the soil is completely dry. Reduce watering in winter. Wrinkles indicate underwatering.

HUMIDITY • Low humidity helps to prevent root rot.

SOIL • Well-draining, coarse succulent mix.

FERTILIZER • Feed sparingly with a low-nitrogen liquid fertilizer once a month at half the manufacturer's recommended rate or less. Star cacti need lots of light if being fed; plants in low-light conditions should receive even less supplemental fertility. Do not feed in winter.

SHOPPING • Star cacti are not carried by every retailer, so scoop up any interesting plants you discover.

POTTING • Repot yearly.

GROWTH • Very slow growing, most star cacti will reach only the size of a softball. Exceptionally old plants can reach 2 feet (0.6 m) in height.

Aloe striata subsp. *karasbergensis*

VARIEGATED WHITE ALOE

IF YOU'VE EVER HAD A BAD SUNBURN, you're likely familiar with aloe vera, the plant known for its use as a skin-soothing balm. But genus *Aloe* extends far beyond its most famous member, containing almost five hundred species of succulents. Though native to the Arabian Peninsula, these sun-worshipping specimens can be found across the globe in a vast array of sizes and appearances.

The classic aloe vera is known for its tall, spiky leaves with toothy edges, but the *Aloe* genus includes more compact dwarf varieties as well as smoother silhouettes. You'll find a wealth of patterns, too; dots, tiger stripes, and more unusual markings make aloes an outstanding choice for introducing visual interest among solid green plants.

Our favorite variety, *Aloe striata* subsp. *karasbergensis*, falls into the category of showily patterned aloes. Its crisp white pinstripes play out over leaves edged with the tiniest of serrations, which bend gracefully backward from a central leader as they grow older. It will develop a tidy shape in full sun, but its striped leaves tend to amble outward in lower light for a wilder silhouette (as pictured at right). Its playful stripes and smooth overall texture also make it exceptionally friendly looking, a pleasing contrast to its pricklier cousins.

Though quite impactful thanks to its variegations, this aloe is relatively small in scale; its maximum size is around 30 inches (76 cm) tall, and it will grow to that height slowly. Its modest stature and approachable presence make it the perfect low-fuss option for any sunny space.

LIGHT • Full sun. At least six hours of direct light daily.

WATER • Minimal. Let the soil dry fully between waterings. Reduce watering in winter. It's normal for lower leaves to turn hard and brown as they age; however, yellow or rotting leaves indicate overwatering.

SOIL • Well-draining, coarse succulent mix.

FERTILIZER • Feed sparingly with a low-nitrogen liquid fertilizer once a month at half the manufacturer's recommended rate or less. Aloes need lots of light if being fed; plants in low-light conditions should receive even less supplemental fertility. Do not feed in winter.

PESTS & DISEASE • Can be susceptible to scale and mealybugs.

SHOPPING • Slow growing indoors; buy the size you want for display.

POTTING • Aloes can have a low, sprawling growth habit; you may see your plant spill from the side of its pot as it matures. This is normal, but you can repot it for additional support.

PROPAGATION • May produce offsets, which can be separated from the mother plant and repotted.

SCULPTURE GARDEN

Wildly varied in appearance but with generally similar care requirements, succulents and cacti are great in groupings: showcase several species together to generate a richly layered effect. Thanks to their elegant curves and myriad hues, prickly pear cacti (*Opuntia*) are especially alluring in this type of collection.

Here, the muted palette of the pots and the addition of rocky top-dressings nod to the opuntia's native home in the desert. (Succulents and cacti can handle rock top-dressings as long as the soil below drains well.) Succulent underplantings infuse additional detail: *Senecio radicans* (commonly called "fishhooks") is a great pairing for large-paddled opuntia, providing textural contrast and helping to regulate water in the pot.

SEVEN

RAMBLERS

VINING & TRAILING PLANTS

W E LOVE VINING AND TRAILING PLANTS FOR THEIR adventurous spirit. They're wanderers, with tiny tendrils forever seeking new places to explore. And they're at home in unusual settings: cascading from lofty perches or ascending shapely structures. Their far-reaching tendencies give them an endless capacity to surprise us as they grow.

When choosing a home for these houseplants, focus on giving them opportunities for that growth; they'll reward you with extraordinary habits if given space to climb or cascade. Trailing plants like hoya (page 176) and string of hearts (page 182) are great options for introducing greenery in unexpected places. Starting from a perch found in your home—perhaps a bookshelf or the top of a cabinet—they'll move through a room in a way that sets them apart from traditional potted houseplants. They're especially striking when encouraged to trail around a mirror; the plant benefits from the additional reflected light, and its greenery will appear multiplied. You can also suspend them in a hanging basket, elevate them with an urn or a plant stand, or use them as a creeping groundcover in an underplanting.

Along with graceful trailing plants, this chapter contains eager vines that thrive when given a structure for support. Like their trailing counterparts, vining specimens offer a look that's distinctive among houseplants. They introduce verticality to your spaces and can be elegantly architectural when paired with a shapely structure.

If you love the look of the vining and trailing plants on the following pages, there are even more options to consider. Turn to page 114 for pothos, a perfect beginner's vine, or to page 54 for vining members of the trendy aroid family.

HOYA

Hoya care varies widely; be sure to research the needs of your specific plant.

LIGHT • Bright indirect light; some varieties burn in full sun.

WATER • Allow the soil to mostly dry between waterings. When in flower, keep blooms dry while watering. Add water until it drains through the soil into the saucer. Wait thirty minutes, then drain any excess water. Leaves will slightly wrinkle or "pucker" when the plant is thirsty. If the foliage develops a yellow cast, the plant is too dry or was left in standing water too long.

HUMIDITY • Benefits from humidity. When in bloom, do not mist flowers.

SOIL • Well-draining potting mix amended with organic matter and orchid bark or other aggregates for added drainage, nutrition, and structure.

FERTILIZER • Apply a balanced liquid fertilizer at half the manufacturer's recommended rate once a month during the growing season (spring to summer), tapering off in fall and ceasing in winter. To encourage flowering, switch to a fertilizer higher in phosphorus.

PESTS & DISEASE • Can be susceptible to mealybugs.

PRUNING • New flowers develop from woody spurs (called peduncles), so never prune or pinch off woody stems.

MAJESTIC AND DAZZLINGLY DIVERSE, the *Hoya* genus is a plant collector's playground. Also known as "wax flowers" or "porcelain flowers," these tropicals hail from Southeast Asia and Australia. Their popularity has grown worldwide, however, thanks to the hundreds of vining and trailing species currently available. Their exceptional collectability has given rise to thriving hoya societies (see page 249), whose members name, collect, and trade their favorite cultivars. If you find yourself falling for hoyas like we have, these groups are a fantastic way to engage with like-minded plant lovers.

Among collectors, hoyas are prized for shape, size, foliage color, and flower fragrance. Though they are generally sturdier and woodier than other vines, their succulent-like foliage varies by cultivar, offering everything from sweetly heart-shaped leaves to broad 6-inch (15 cm) paddles. They bloom repeatedly, and their flowers are striking: fragrant clusters of downward-facing umbels with the texture of dewy porcelain.

Encouraging a hoya to bloom is a waiting game; they flower only after reaching a certain point in maturity. In the meantime, there's plenty to appreciate about their foliage. Easy-to-find yet lovely options include *Hoya curtisii* (pictured opposite) and *H. carnosa* 'Krimson Queen', with tricolor foliage in green, pink, and white. Varieties that are less frequently produced in the broader plant market (like *H. aldrichii*, pictured at left) can be found at specialty growers like Gardino Nursery (see page 188). Also consider *H. kerrii*, often sold as a single heart-shaped paddle around Valentine's Day. (These grocery store novelties don't have enough roots for future growth, however; it's worth finding a full-size plant to enjoy more of its charming leaves.)

Good beginner's houseplants, hoyas are generally sturdy and tough to kill—but there are exceptions. Because the genus is so diverse, care requirements vary widely; some varieties are hardy, others quite fussy. We've provided general guidelines at left, but be sure to research the needs of your particular plant. Because their light and water requirements are often quite specific, they're best displayed as stand-alone "pets" rather than grown in a mixed planting. Try showcasing your hoya in an urn or a hanging basket to spotlight its form and—someday!—its flowers.

DISCHIDIA

WE FIRST FELL IN LOVE WITH DISCHIDIA in Thailand, where we spotted it hanging in curtains from tree branches, much like Spanish moss in the southern United States. Relatives of the hoya (page 176) that hail from tropical China, India, and Southeast Asia, dischidias are returning to the US plant market after a long absence—and we're thrilled to be part of their comeback.

Dischidias are all-around fantastic foliage plants, with fleshy, succulent-like leaves that are less tender than the typical tropical leaf. Their stems are stiff yet thin, and their blooms are tiny—selection here is all about your foliage preference. Though most often grown as pendulous, trailing plants, they will climb if given a support structure. They're easygoing when it comes to care, adaptable to a variety of light conditions, and forgiving of any mistake except overwatering.

Genus *Dischidia* is a designer's wonderland, filled with great diversity in leaf color, texture, and shape. For a classic look with slightly elongated leaves, seek out lime-green *D. oiantha* 'Cascade' and its variegated cultivar *D. oiantha* 'Variegata' (shown here), which features mint-green foliage with white margins. Available in solid green and variegated varieties, *D. ruscifolia* (nicknamed "million hearts") is coated in tiny heart-shaped leaves. *D. nummularia*, commonly called "string of nickels," offers round, fleshy leaves, some with a slightly pointed shape. Most unusual, *D. pectinoides* produces balloon-like foliage; in the wild, its leaves house the ants that pollinate the plant.

No matter which cultivar you choose, dischidias are excellent for any climbing or trailing design application. Because they have care requirements similar to those of many typical succulents, they also offer a planting option that's uncommon among tropical vines: they can grow alongside succulents in a mixed container. Encourage the vines to trail over the side of the vessel and create an intriguing intersection of two worlds: the tropical forest and the sun-washed desert.

LIGHT • Bright indirect light; will grow in full sun, though foliage color may become bleached out.

WATER • Water when the soil becomes dry.

HUMIDITY • Benefits from humidity.

SOIL • Well-draining potting mix amended with organic matter and orchid bark or other aggregates for added drainage, nutrition, and structure.

FERTILIZER • Apply a balanced liquid fertilizer at half the manufacturer's recommended rate once a month during the growing season (spring to summer), tapering off in fall and ceasing in winter.

VINING & TRAILING SUCCULENTS

LIGHT • Bright direct to indirect light; place near a sunny window, but avoid direct sun to prevent burning.

WATER • Let the soil dry between waterings, but never so much that it shrinks away from the edge of the pot. A weekly schedule usually works well in spring and summer. In winter, water every two or three weeks. Shriveled leaves and a die-off of new growth indicate underwatering; squishy yellow leaves and thinning near the soil line indicate overwatering.

SOIL • Lightweight succulent mix (add peat or coconut coir if you have a heavier blend).

FERTILIZER • Apply a balanced liquid fertilizer at half the manufacturer's recommended rate once a month during the growing season (spring to summer), tapering off in fall and ceasing in winter.

SHOPPING • Buy these slow growers close to your desired size.

POTTING • Choose a clay pot with ample drainage. Most of these plants won't develop deep roots, so select a shallow vessel, right-sized for the plant, and keep the crown of the plant level with the rim to prevent water pooling near the roots.

WE'VE DEDICATED A FULL CHAPTER to the quirky charms of terrestrial succulents (see chapter six), but vining and trailing succulents can differ substantially from their relatives in both appearance and care. Scattered across the plant kingdom yet united by their cascading growth, these species are among the most compelling in the plant world: tactile, exceedingly delicate, and guaranteed to stop you in your tracks.

Most are native to arid climates in southern Africa, so these succulents will decline if their soil is constantly moist or if left to dry out completely during the growing season. The good news is, they'll tell you when they're unhappy; you just have to spot the signs of distress in time (see left).

Their intriguing textures and silhouettes make them stunning stand-alone specimens; let them shine in a tall urn, hanging basket, or pot on a high shelf. They can also be paired with one another to create wonderfully textural mixed plantings. Finally, we like to use them as an underplanting for upright succulents and cacti (as shown on pages 172–173); their light requirements are similar, and they can help to regulate water in the container.

Their outstanding versatility has made these succulents very popular among houseplant lovers, so commercial growers are frequently introducing lesser-known cultivars to market. In our specimen guide on the following pages, you'll see familiar species like string of pearls and *Senecio* varieties that have been in the market for a long time, as well as lesser-known options such as the silver dollar vine (pictured at left) that are gaining in popularity.

VINING & TRAILING SUCCULENTS

Senecio rowleyanus f. *variegatus*
Variegated string of pearls

A classic that never goes out of style, this trailing species' long chains of perfect orbs are compellingly tactile but also delicate; its leaves are weighty compared to the slender stems, so handle gently to avoid knocking them off. With proper care, the chains can reach 4 feet (1.2 m) in length. Solid green plants are widely available; keep an eye out for this variegated version, *Senecio rowleyanus* f. *variegatus*. In addition, look for related cultivars, each one expressively named by leaf shape: *S. radicans*, known as "string of bananas," and *S. peregrinus*, called "string of dolphins."

Ceropegia woodii
String of hearts

This species infuses the scale and trailing silhouette of "string of pearls" with an airy charm, because its heart-shaped leaves hang from the stems at an angle. As new colors come to market, *C. woodii* has become a collector's favorite. The most common variety (shown here) has dappled, mint-green leaves; harder-to-find options include frosty 'Silver Glory', as well as variegated cultivars.

Othonna capensis
'Ruby Necklace'

This newer-to-market cultivar is also sold as "string of rubies" or "string of pickles." Its prolific stems sprout pickle-shaped leaves for a dense, unruly silhouette, but its true standout feature is its color. The stems are a soft purple, while the leaves transform from green to reddish purple in bright sun (limit exposure at the height of summer to prevent burning). We love 'Ruby Necklace' spilling from a mixed planter, where it provides a vivid splash of color and texture.

Xerosicyos danguyi
Silver dollar vine

An in-demand favorite among houseplant enthusiasts, the silver dollar vine has a more rigid habit than many cascading options. Its woody stems grow upright before eventually cascading, and produce tiny, curly tendrils that can aid in climbing. Sturdy leaves in the shape of flattened circles perch along the stems, creating an intriguing overall silhouette. This vine is best displayed as a stand-alone specimen; pair it with a pole or hoop to support its weighty branches.

Muehlenbeckia complexa

ANGEL VINE

DISTINCTIVELY DELICATE, this easy-to-find plant offers a look that's quite different from other vines. Tiny oval or round leaves seem to hover above its exceedingly fine stems, giving the angel vine a lacy aesthetic that's ever more beguiling as it grows. (And it will grow, quickly!) Though the plant will form a dense mat as it spreads, the dainty stems and leaves maintain an airy feel.

This vigorous grower can be trained on almost any structure that provides an open framework. Try pairing this vine with an obelisk or a tuteur, juxtaposing its delicate botanical detail with a highly architectural silhouette. You can also experiment with simpler, handmade wire supports because angel vine is so lightweight— see an example on page 223.

While striking when grown on a form, this versatile vine can also be used as a trailing groundcover. (Native to highlands in Australia and New Zealand, it's actually hardy enough to grow as outdoor groundcover in Zones 6 and 7 of the United States.) Plant it below an upright specimen like an autograph tree (page 205) to fill the surface area in a larger container. Thanks to its exquisitely intricate texture, a solo angel vine also offers ample interest when simply allowed to fill an elevated pot, especially in its variegated form, *M. complexa* 'Tricolor' (as shown here).

LIGHT • Bright indirect light. Can tolerate full sun, but then be sure to keep soil consistently moist.

WATER • Angel vines are sensitive to underwatering. In full sun to very bright light, the soil should be kept evenly moist; water until it drains from the pot at least once a week. In lower-light conditions, allow the top 2 inches (5 cm) of soil to dry before watering, then water until it drains from the pot.

HUMIDITY • Benefits from misting.

SOIL • Rich, well-draining potting mix.

FERTILIZER • In the growing season (spring to fall), feed with a balanced liquid fertilizer once a month at half the manufacturer's recommended rate. When plant growth slows in winter, stop fertilizing.

PRUNING • Regular pruning can increase growth, directing energy away from new tendrils and back to the main body of the plant. Trim to your desired shape once or twice a year.

A CASCADING COLLECTION

A bookshelf is a lovely place to showcase a group of vining and trailing plants, providing ample opportunity for tendrils to travel. This setup is especially good for plants that share similar light requirements; a shelf oriented near a window makes it easier to care for—and enjoy—the grouping.

When arranging a collection of plants on a bookshelf, consider form, balance, and negative space. Leave room for each plant to vine or cascade. Think about variety, too; sinuous spills of foliage are even more arresting when shown in contrast to self-contained specimens. Highly collectible thanks to their exceptional diversity, hoyas are perfect for this type of wild yet contained display. To create quiet moments among the plants, you might scatter some decorative objects—like the pieces of pottery shown here—throughout the shelves.

GARDINO NURSERY

LOXAHATCHEE GROVES, FLORIDA

"You might say I was chosen by a bean," Sid Gardino quips about his lifelong love for plants. "When I was around four years old, my teacher asked all the students to bring in a bean to plant. She said the first to sprout would indicate who was best in the class. A couple of days later, my bean was first! For a little kid, that sprout was important.

"I was always outside, messing with plants," Sid says of his childhood. He and his wife, Regina, grew up in Brazil, where they experienced the plant mania that swept the country in the 1970s. Some ferns, particularly the majestic *Polypodium subauriculatum,* became so coveted that collectors would steal them from one another. "I got really into ferns, collecting and trading them," recalls Sid. "Once I had that little collection, I fell in love with orchids. Around the same time, my mother gave me a houseplant book: *Viva o Verde* by Rob Herwig. I basically memorized it. There are times now when I see a plant and still remember its name from that book."

As Sid's interest continued to develop, he began growing specimens to sell at plant shows. Economic challenges in Brazil eventually prompted Sid and Regina to move to the United States, where the couple started their Florida nursery in 1994. Four years ago, they moved to a 5-acre (2 ha) property where they cultivate thousands of species, including ferns, aroids, orchids, flowering trees, gingers, and Regina's specialty: hoyas.

"I started collecting hoyas around 1998," Regina recalls. "We already had a couple of common varieties like *carnosa* and *bella,* but then we went to a plant show and I saw so many with different

On their property, the Gardinos have created both indoor and outdoor growing spaces. The hoyas are all grown inside; hardier species can be found in shaded outdoor areas.

leaves. I said to Sid, 'I love them!' but he didn't think they did well in Florida. I decided to try anyway, and they grew really well." From there, Regina's collection multiplied to over four hundred species and cultivars. The nursery's reputation as a source for remarkable hoyas grew, too.

When hoyas skyrocketed in popularity around 2008, the Gardinos had already been selling them online for several years. "We started on eBay with rare hoyas," says the couple's daughter, Paula. "Then we began selling via our website around 2000. Now we have a dedicated greenhouse for hoyas, and people come to shop by appointment." The nursery even has four of their own hybrids, which have occurred naturally over the years. "Hoyas are very difficult to pollinate," says Sid. "The reproductive parts are so small that you need jeweler's lenses to

work. So we watch for natural hybrids, then select and keep the best ones."

Today, Paula is following in her mother's footsteps. "I've gotten really into hoyas," she says. "They're so easy and there are so many varieties!" Regina adds, "Sometimes I say that Paula knows more than me. I find myself asking her for names."

Part of hoyas' widespread appeal is their diversity, with vining, trailing, and shrub-like options in an array of leaf shapes and colors. "Many people choose them for the beauty of their leaves," says Regina. "Hoyas

---

ABOVE: Sid, Paula, and Regina outside a hoya house. "I'm in charge of weekly restocks of hoya," says Paula. "I have some orchids at home, too, but hoyas are the most fun!" OPPOSITE, CLOCKWISE FROM TOP: A row of mother plants hangs in one of the nursery's grow houses; *Hoya* aff. *clemensiorum* IML 1752; *H. latifolia* IML 1590 (formerly H. *aff. clandestina*).

bloom all the time here in Florida, but people up north grow them indoors, where conditions are less ideal for blooming, so pretty leaves are preferred." The Gardinos have seen unusual colors become especially popular, with pink speckles, silver flecks, and bold variegations in high demand.

Though the Florida climate helps their hoyas bloom, it brings challenges, too. Some hoyas are native to mountain climates with hot, humid days and cool nights. In the unrelenting heat of Floridian summers, explains Regina, "they just melt." Florida winters do have temperatures low enough for the hoyas to develop vibrant colors, which are a stress response to chilly conditions. "We see lots of reds and oranges in the greenhouse during winter," she says.

The Gardinos describe their hoya house as a riotous space, especially during summer when the plants' roving tendrils grow at a measurable rate each day. "The tendrils will wrap around anything they touch," says Sid. "In the hoya house, they grab your coat, they grab your glasses, they tangle together . . ."

Hoyas' clingy nature hasn't deterred countless collectors in the plant community, which is thriving more than ever thanks to connections made online. The internet has also changed the way people learn about plant care. "We used to have long descriptions on the website," Regina and Paula explain. "But now customers prefer to ask questions on Facebook. With the internet and plant clubs, they ask each other, too." The Gardinos do provide basic care instructions with

OPPOSITE: A selection of small rooted hoya plants available for purchase. The Gardinos open one hoya house, seen here, to the public for shopping by appointment. Turn the page for a wider view. ABOVE: Hoya 'Patricia' (*H. darwinii* x *H. elliptica*) in bloom.

their plants and note particular needs, but Sid thinks learning is its own reward. "Even after forty-six years, I still buy plants on impulse, then learn how to grow them. That's part of the fun!"

Having lived through the houseplant crazes of the 1970s and the internet age, Regina and Sid reflect on the differences and similarities: "In Brazil during the seventies, one fern, *Polypodium subauriculatum*, started it all. Then people asked, 'What other ferns are there?' That was the pattern with later waves of popular plants like orchids and bonsai, too. The difference now is the internet. Plant fevers spread faster, and all around the world."

Since they've seen trends come and go, the Gardinos make sure they offer a diverse assortment of plants. "Sometimes everyone wants ferns, then it's orchids, then it's cacti and succulents," says Sid. "Hoyas and aroids became popular at the same time. Maybe in a few years, no one will care about hoyas." Regina quickly counters, "Hoyas will be forever!"

Will Gardino Nursery be forever? "You never know how the market will be," says Sid. "We've had rough times. At the start of the pandemic, we were really scared. But when people started staying home and buying plants, business exploded." Their current location has room for only a few more greenhouses. If the business continues growing, they may need to look for more land. For now, they'll keep stocking all types of plants, so they always have something to sell.

Just like the next plant trend, the future of the nursery is unpredictable, particularly as Sid and Regina get older. But Paula is ready to carry on her parents' legacy. "This wasn't always my plan," she says, "but I grew up in the nursery and going to plant shows. Little by little, I got more into plants, and became obsessed with hoyas. We have a good thing going here, and I'll keep it going as long as I can."

RIGHT: This hoya house is open to the public for shopping by appointment. Because hoyas are so slow to bloom, the Gardinos carefully catalog and display images of each plant's flower for customers to view.

EIGHT

DRAMA CLASS

TREES, PALMS &

OTHER STATEMENT SPECIMENS

T HANKS TO THEIR GRAND SCALE AND ABUNDANT FOLIAGE, these plants have the power to create a magical green canopy that will flourish above and around you. The big, bold specimens in this chapter present design opportunities no other houseplants can offer.

The popular *Ficus lyrata* has dominated the world of large-scale houseplants for some time. While this trendy tree offers foliage of superb shape and size, it's exceptionally fussy and has become a ubiquitous decor piece. In its place, we've curated two lesser-known ficus options—*Ficus* 'Audrey' (page 198) and ficus triangularis (page 210)—that are equally remarkable and easier to care for. These options provide a tantalizing glimpse into the diversity of the genus; the former echoes the classic tree form of *F. lyrata*, while the latter possesses a shrubby silhouette.

While an upright tree like a ficus might be the most obvious choice when you want to bring a showstopping houseplant into your home, you can also make a splash with extra-large leaves and eye-catching habits. Consider the broad fronds of a licuala (page 202), or the charmingly irregular shape of *Clusia rosea* (page 205), both substantial and intriguing enough to stand alone as a showpiece or anchor a collection of smaller plants. Drama takes many forms, so find the plant that's right for your space, then allow it to transport a lush natural world indoors.

Ficus benghalensis 'Audrey'

FICUS 'AUDREY'

FICUS 'AUDREY' is the national tree of India, and it's easy to see why it was chosen. This tropical native of Southeast Asia has a regal presence thanks to its elegant shape, considerable scale, and textural interest.

If you're searching for an indoor tree with a traditional trunk-and-canopy silhouette (called a standard form, or STD, in the industry), 'Audrey' is an excellent pick. You can sometimes find a bushy 2- or 3-foot (0.6 or 0.9 m) specimen, but it's most often sold in larger tree forms. (You'll see both tightly pruned and unpruned trees in the market; we prefer the wilder, unpruned shape shown here.) *Ficus* 'Audrey' has broad leaves with pronounced veining and a fuzzy texture, offering a tactile interest not found in other ficus varieties. The leaves are also distinctively colored, with deep green surfaces and whitish gray undersides for an attractively stark look. Light conditions in your home will change your tree's aesthetic; direct light will encourage a fuller, leafier silhouette, while indirect light yields a more open habit.

'Audrey' is our pick for those who love *F. lyrata*'s showy foliage but are burned out by its finicky nature. Some would argue that 'Audrey' is also fussy, but it can be easy to care for: just remember that it loves routine. When you bring your plant home, choose a permanent location with a steady temperature (no drafts), then establish a watering schedule. Once you understand its needs, *Ficus* 'Audrey' will thrive.

LIGHT • Bright indirect light or direct morning sun; can't tolerate direct afternoon sun.

WATER • 'Audrey' is sensitive to over- and underwatering and prefers room-temperature water. Water thoroughly when the top 2 inches (5 cm) of soil become dry, pouring in water until it drains into the saucer. After thirty minutes, drain any excess water; use a turkey baster if the plant is too heavy to lift.

SOIL • Well-draining potting mix amended with orchid bark and other aggregates for added drainage and support.

FERTILIZER • Apply nitrogen-rich slow-release granular indoor fertilizer every four months from spring to early fall, skipping winter. Follow the manufacturer's instructions. If the plant shows acute nutrient distress (leaf drop and discoloration) between feedings, apply dilute liquid fertilizer every third watering until distress abates.

PESTS & DISEASE • Though 'Audrey' is generally pest resistant, scale can be an issue.

SHOPPING • Slow growing; for an instant statement piece, purchase a more established plant.

POTTING • Mature leaves reach 8 to 9 inches (20 to 23 cm) long; if your plant starts producing smaller leaves, repot in a larger container.

Bucida buceras 'Shady Lady'

BLACK OLIVE TREE

A STANDOUT AMONG INDOOR TREES thanks to its delicate texture and architectural shape, *Bucida buceras* 'Shady Lady' is a slender specimen with a more petite leaf form than you usually see in plants of this size.

Though known as the "black olive tree," *B. buceras* isn't an olive at all. (It *can* bear olive-like fruit in summer or fall, but the fruit is inedible and doesn't always appear indoors.) It's actually a native of tropical Central and South America, where it grows in coastal swamps and wet inland forests, often along riverbanks—so be sure to establish a good watering routine.

We love 'Shady Lady' primarily for its pleasing habit. Its horizontal branches create an orderly, striated effect, and the plant stays fairly narrow as it grows, eschewing the top-heavy "lollipop" silhouette common among indoor trees. Dainty leaves also lend it a lovely texture, refreshing in contrast to the broad-leaved look of many larger-scale houseplants.

This tidy appearance makes 'Shady Lady' well suited for adding formality and structure to a space. You'll usually find it sold as a tall, slender tree, making it particularly good for smaller rooms with high ceilings. Consider placing it in a corner, where its narrow silhouette and well-dispersed branches will fill the space but not feel overbearing. Its upright form can also emphasize architectural elements when used to frame a window, doorway, or fireplace. A credit to its ladylike name, it's a subtle and elegant addition to the world of statement houseplants.

LIGHT • Bright direct light. Can be adapted to some indirect light (see page 21).

WATER • Water once a week, pouring in water until it drains into the saucer. After thirty minutes, drain any excess water; use a turkey baster if the plant is too heavy to lift.

SOIL • Well-draining potting mix amended with orchid bark and other aggregates for added drainage and support.

FERTILIZER • Apply a slow-release granular indoor fertilizer every four to six months from spring to early fall, skipping winter. Follow the manufacturer's instructions for rates and application. If the plant shows acute nutrient distress (leaf drop and discoloration) between granular feedings, sparingly apply a balanced liquid fertilizer every third watering until distress abates.

TEMPERATURE • 'Shady Lady' is extremely cold sensitive; even placing it temporarily on cold pavement can be detrimental. Avoid drafts and temperatures below 50°F (10°C).

GROWTH • Specimens are usually offered as 6- to 9-foot (1.8 to 2.7 m) trees and grow slowly.

PRUNING • Prune as needed in spring to maintain shape, removing any heavy upper branches.

Licuala

GIANT FAN PALM

THE GIANT FAN PALM has long been one of our particular fascinations. This tropical treasure stands apart from other palms in both appearance and care: its massive leaves are extraordinarily eye-catching, while its undemanding nature makes the verdant look of a palm accessible indoors.

Let's start with the licuala's most notable feature: those fronds! Giant fan palms boast broad leaves, which can either be solid and umbrellalike or have a split silhouette. Each leaf emerges over the course of several months from a central clump of stems, rewarding patient observers with graphic planes of greenery. These palms can reach a sprawling 8 to 10 feet (2.4 to 3 m) tall and 6 feet (1.8 m) wide, the epitome of tropical drama. Mature trees are large enough to anchor a room alone, but they will also tolerate sharing their pot with an underplanting; try a smaller-scale aroid that shares their tropical aesthetic and care requirements, like *Epipremnum pinnatum* (pages 116–117).

Though large by houseplant standards, licualas are understory dwellers in the jungles of Southeast Asia. This makes them great candidates for growing indoors, because they don't require the intense sunlight that other palms need. In addition, the shelter of indoor spaces protects their delicate fronds from inclement weather, which often shreds them.

Licualas are slow growing, limited in availability, and commensurately expensive. Don't be put off by the price—you can invest without trepidation in these sturdy specimens. We love the majestic scale of *L. peltata* var. *sumawongii* (pictured opposite and on pages 214–215). *L. grandis* offers the same look at a more compact height (5 to 6 feet/1.5 to 1.8 m) and narrower width. *L. ramsayi* (left) is another delightful option; its fronds split as it grows, forming natural pinwheels. Native to Australia, *ramsayi* offers the height and clumping habit of a *sumawongii* with a more intricate divided-frond look.

LIGHT • Bright indirect light. Can tolerate one to two hours of direct sun; avoid all-day exposure.

WATER • Keep the soil generally moist, watering when the top 1 to 2 inches (2.5 to 5 cm) become dry. After thirty minutes, drain any excess water; use a turkey baster if the plant is too heavy to lift.

HUMIDITY • Requires humidity. Watch for brown leaf tips, which indicate that the humidity is too low.

SOIL • Well-draining potting mix amended with organic matter and orchid bark for added drainage and nutrition.

FERTILIZER • Apply slow-release granular fertilizer specific to palms every four months from spring to late summer, skipping fall and winter. Follow the manufacturer's instructions. If the plant shows acute nutrient distress (leaf drop and discoloration) between feedings, apply dilute liquid fertilizer every third watering until distress abates.

PESTS & DISEASE • Can be susceptible to scale.

SHOPPING • Licualas are usually sold in 12- to 14-inch (30 to 36 cm) pots. They're slow growing, so buy close to your desired size.

Clusia rosea

AUTOGRAPH TREE

IF YOU'RE NEW TO THE WORLD OF TREES as houseplants, *Clusia rosea* is a rewarding first foray into the category, sturdy and striking in equal measure. This subtropical stunner is nicknamed the autograph tree because you can etch permanent markings into its leathery leaves, but it has plenty of visual interest without additions from budding artists. This robust plant is native to Florida and the Caribbean, where it's often used as an outdoor hedge, similar in function to a boxwood. It's equally at home, however, as a character-packed, low-maintenance indoor plant.

C. *rosea* can be cultivated as a tree with an upright ball-and-stem silhouette, but it's commonly grown as a woody shrub. We prefer the shrub for its irregular, charmingly informal shape, which is much rangier than that of the other plants in this chapter. It grows up to 10 feet (3 m) tall indoors, covered with thick, succulent-like leaves that can be solid or variegated (as shown here). Solid leaves offer a cheerful burst of greenery, but we especially love the high-contrast, cream-colored margins of the variegated form.

In the wild, C. *rosea* can grow as an epiphyte, sprouting atop rocks and gathering moisture and nutrients from air and water alone. This makes it hardier than many indoor trees, especially when it comes to moisture; the autograph tree can tolerate a missed watering as long as it's not allowed to dry out completely or subjected to excess moisture. An underplanting like the one pictured opposite (angel vine, page 185), can help regulate water evaporation.

LIGHT • Bright direct light is ideal. If placed in indirect light, C. *rosea* will put out fewer leaves, creating a more open silhouette.

WATER • Water when the soil becomes lightly dry. Drain any excess water from the saucer; use a turkey baster if the plant is too heavy to lift.

HUMIDITY • Requires humidity. Mist occasionally.

SOIL • Well-draining potting mix amended with orchid bark and other aggregates for added drainage and support.

FERTILIZER • Apply nitrogen-rich slow-release granular indoor fertilizer every four months from spring to early fall, skipping winter. Follow the manufacturer's instructions for rates and application. If the plant shows acute nutrient distress (leaf drop and discoloration) between granular feedings, apply a dilute liquid fertilizer every third watering until distress abates.

TEMPERATURE • C. *rosea* prefers temperatures above 50 to 55°F (10 to 13°C), but can withstand drafts.

SHOPPING • You can find both small- and large-leaved varieties; smaller leaves measure 2 to 3 inches (5 to 8 cm), while larger ones measure 4 to 5 inches (10 to 13 cm).

ELEPHANT EAR PLANT

STURDY AND REWARDING, elephant ear plants are instantly recognizable for their giant, heart-shaped foliage, offering an exaggerated form that's not commonly seen in houseplants. In northern climes, they are most often grown from bulbs as outdoor annuals, but we adore using them for dramatic flair indoors.

In the wild, the alocasia grows as an understory plant in Southeast Asia. Rooted in the rich soil of the forest floor, the trees above shelter its massive leaves from wind damage. Because its native habitat provides dappled sunlight, it's a great statement plant for spaces with indirect lighting.

Recent genetic developments have added lots of playful new options to this well-established genus; you can find everything from modest tabletop plants to 6-foot (1.8 m) showstoppers, with a wide range of colors and textures to explore. To give smaller specimens additional presence, elevate them on a stand or a tall urn, so you can walk beneath their leaves. Regardless of size, all alocasias share a similar habit: several stems fan outward from a central clump, supporting a sprawling canopy of foliage. And they share similar, relatively manageable care requirements.

Within the genus, two exceptional alocasias stand out. If you'd like a tall and broad plant, consider *Alocasia* 'Dark Star' (pictured at left), which features solid green leaves with black stems and ribbing. Four to 6 feet (1.2 to 1.8 m) tall at maturity, it's a high-contrast option that's especially spectacular in light-walled rooms. If you prefer a more modest and narrower silhouette, try *A. zebrina* 'Tigrina Superba' (pictured opposite), which packs lots of interest into a moderate 4-foot (1.2 m) height. Textural, zebra-striped stems support linear, arrow-shaped leaves that appear solid green but hold a surprise: backlighting reveals the secret, swirling pattern of their veins.

LIGHT • Bright indirect light; burns in full sun. Alocasia can suffer from low light in winter. If the light decreases significantly, move the plant to a brighter location.

WATER • Water when the top 2 to 3 inches (5 to 8 cm) of soil become dry. After thirty minutes, drain excess water from the saucer; use a turkey baster if the plant is too heavy to lift. Reduce frequency slightly in winter. Alocasia leaves "sweat" excess water, a process called guttation. A few drops are normal; lots of moisture indicates overwatering. Additional signs of overwatering include mushiness in new growth or at the plant's center.

HUMIDITY • Thrives in humidity.

SOIL • Well-draining potting mix amended with organic matter and orchid bark for added drainage and nutrition.

FERTILIZER • In the growing season (spring to fall), feed with a balanced liquid fertilizer every two weeks at half the manufacturer's recommended rate. When plant growth slows in winter, stop fertilizing.

PESTS & DISEASE • Susceptible to spider mites, which misting helps prevent. Overwatering can cause fungal issues, which appear as spots on the leaves.

SHOPPING • Growing from bulbs is slow indoors; it's best to purchase a mature plant if you're looking for statement size.

PRUNING • Cut older leaves away from the base as they die off (as shown on page 28).

Strelitzia nicolai

GIANT WHITE BIRD-OF-PARADISE

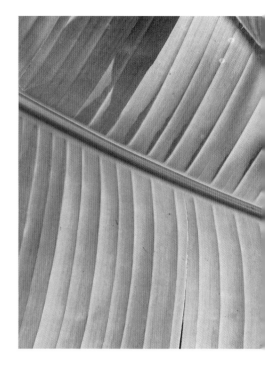

MANY MIGHT KNOW BIRD-OF-PARADISE as a bird-shaped orange flower found in gardens across Mexico and in warm, sunny regions of the United States (in addition to in its native habitat of tropical South Africa). Its oversize relative, the giant white bird-of-paradise, makes for an excellent statement houseplant. If you're intimidated by large-scale tropicals but love their look, *Strelitzia nicolai* is a friendly introduction to the category. It has lots of leafy drama, grows quickly and without fuss, and is likely available at your local nursery for an affordable price—all the makings of a great "bang for your buck" houseplant.

Unlike its orange cousin, this bird-of-paradise is all about foliage. It's sometimes called "wild banana," a name inspired by the broad, paddle-shaped leaves that mimic a banana tree's classic tropical aesthetic. The leaves grow in an upright fan, quickly gaining height as they branch from a central base. A mature bird-of-paradise can reach 12 feet (3.6 m) or taller indoors, offering the size of a tree with a less-rigid form. Like licuala (page 202), this plant benefits from a pampered indoor life; its leaves easily shred outside but stay pristine when sheltered from the elements.

Those large leaves give *S. nicolai* a fantastic and versatile presence. It quickly reaches the size needed to become the focal point of a room; in especially large spaces, arrange several plants in a line to create a living divider. Though it has the stature to stand alone, it also works well with an underplanting of *Ficus repens* (as shown opposite).

LIGHT • Minimum of four hours of bright direct light daily, or all-day bright indirect light. Rotate periodically if the light comes from one side only.

WATER • Keep the soil generally moist, watering when the top 1 to 2 inches (2.5 to 5 cm) become dry. After thirty minutes, drain any excess water; use a turkey baster if the plant is too heavy to lift.

HUMIDITY • Benefits from humidity.

SOIL • Well-draining potting mix amended with organic matter and orchid bark for added drainage and nutrition.

FERTILIZER • In the growing season (spring to fall), feed with a balanced liquid fertilizer every two weeks at half the manufacturer's recommended rate. When plant growth slows in winter, stop fertilizing.

TEMPERATURE • Avoid cold drafts.

PESTS & DISEASE • Susceptible to scale, mealybugs, and spider mites.

SHOPPING • *S. nicolai* are fast growing. For immediate floor-plant scale, look for 10- or 12-inch (25 to 30 cm) pots, which usually contain 3- to 5-foot (0.9 to 1.5 m) plants.

PRUNING • Can prune to manage height. If older leaves droop, trim them away; this returns energy to the plant.

Ficus natalensis subsp. *leprieurii*

FICUS TRIANGULARIS

THIS NEW, LESSER-KNOWN VARIETY from tropical Africa is a modern addition to the enduringly popular *Ficus* genus. *F. natalensis* pairs a substantial scale with an airy aesthetic, perfect for adding height and dimension in spaces that can't support a heavy green presence. Its care is easy (especially in comparison to other ficuses), its form is breezy, and its effect is breathtaking.

Ficus triangularis (pictured at left) is aptly named for its triangular leaves, which are a dark, glossy emerald green. (For the same leaf shape with a green-and-cream coloration, look for the variegated form shown opposite, which also boasts a more upright habit than its solid green counterpart.) The leaves sprout from wiry black stems, which respond well to extra support from a structure while they're young and flexible, so you can train your plant into an upright or arching form as desired. The ficus's open shape prevents it from overwhelming a space, though you may need to prune to maintain your desired height (these trees can grow upward of 80 feet/24 m tall!). And in spite of its wispy appearance, this ficus is surprisingly hardy. It's sensitive to overwatering but otherwise easygoing, and its leathery foliage is sturdily attached, so you won't experience the leaf drop issues common among small-leaved ficus.

Because each stem is so fine, you'll often find ficus triangularis planted as a clump of multiples; this initial planting determines the density of the mature plant. Select a grouping of several stems for a fuller display of foliage, or choose a cluster of just two or three for a delicate look. You can pair ficus triangularis with an underplanting, but you don't need to; it offers ample interest all the way up its stem. A well-balanced silhouette also means you can display an immature plant on a stand or stool without fear that it will topple over.

Along with offering an outstanding form, this ficus excels at adding movement to indoor spaces. Its petite leaves perch lightly atop its stems, perfectly poised to catch even the slightest breeze. If your home has good airflow, the tiny leaves will flutter to life— a truly delightful sight.

LIGHT • Bright direct light. Can be adapted to some indirect light (see page 21).

WATER • Water only when the soil is completely dry, pouring in water until it drains through the soil into the saucer. After thirty minutes, drain any excess water; use a turkey baster if the plant is too heavy to lift. *F. natalensis* is extremely sensitive to overwatering; if the top of the soil stays too moist, the leaves will rot.

HUMIDITY • Thrives in humidity.

SOIL • Well-draining potting mix.

FERTILIZER • Apply a nitrogen-rich slow-release granular indoor fertilizer every four months from spring to early fall, skipping winter. Follow the manufacturer's instructions for rates and application. If the plant shows acute nutrient distress (leaf drop and discoloration) between granular feedings, apply a dilute liquid fertilizer every third watering until distress abates.

TEMPERATURE • This tropical species requires temperatures over 55°F (13°C). To encourage more growth, try moving your plant outdoors during the warm summer months.

PESTS & DISEASE • *F. natalensis* is susceptible to scale.

Citrus × limon 'Eureka Variegated Pink'

VARIEGATED PINK LEMON

CITRUS TREES have long been popular indoor plants. From the seventeenth to nineteenth centuries, fashionable homes often included orangeries: lavish greenhouses where tender fruit trees could grow throughout the year. But you don't need a dedicated greenhouse to enjoy the charms of indoor citrus. While any citrus species will brighten your home with its year-round foliage and cheerful winter fruit, we're particularly enamored of the variegated pink lemon.

Though citrus trees are native to South Asia, this cultivar was discovered in California as a natural sport (mutation) of a Eureka lemon. And when it comes to variegation, this lively lemon is double the fun: the leaves are randomly patterned in cream and green, while the fruit is striped in yellow and green. (Cut into the fruit to reveal bright pink flesh, which has a deliciously mild flavor.) At a mature size of 8 to 12 feet (2.4 to 3.6 m) tall and 6 to 8 feet (1.8 to 2.4 m) wide, it also has the scale to be a centerpiece in your home.

Though its leaves are a year-round delight, you'll also enjoy following your citrus tree throughout its fruiting cycle. It will produce fragrant blooms in spring, begin developing fruit in summer, and become especially impressive during the fall and winter months as the colorful lemons ripen. Because lemon plants are self-pollinating, your tree will fruit indoors. To increase its yield, however, you can do a few things to encourage pollination: place it outside during the summer months or hand-pollinate it indoors; try misting the flower clusters with water, shaking them gently as they open to dislodge and spread pollen, or dabbing multiple open flowers with a paintbrush to deposit pollen around the tree.

One important note about these lovely trees: they need bright direct sunlight throughout the day to thrive. In return, they'll reward you with an abundance of color and a bounty of fresh fruit during winter's darkest days.

LIGHT • Bright direct all-day sun.

WATER • Citrus trees are highly sensitive to overwatering and need consistency. Following repotting, water daily for the first month; after this, water when the top 2 to 3 inches (5 to 8 cm) of soil become dry. After thirty minutes, drain excess water from the saucer; use a turkey baster if the plant is too heavy to lift. Increase watering frequency in very hot conditions. Reduce in winter to once every two weeks.

HUMIDITY • Benefits from humidity.

SOIL • Well-draining potting mix amended with organic matter, sand, and orchid bark for added drainage and nutrition.

FERTILIZER • Apply slow-release granular fertilizer specific to citrus every four months from spring to late summer, skipping fall and winter. Follow the manufacturer's instructions. If the plant shows acute nutrient distress (leaf drop and discoloration) between feedings, apply dilute liquid fertilizer every third watering until distress abates. If the fruit is to be eaten, choose organic fertilizer.

PESTS & DISEASE • Susceptible to scale.

PRUNING • Usually sold in a standard tree form; prune to maintain shape.

CREATING
A CANOPY

Large houseplants, like the licualas shown here, create opportunities to play with scale. These specimens can transform an entire room—but the room itself doesn't have to be large. One substantial plant can make a compact space feel inviting and intimate or fill an empty corner where furniture doesn't fit. In more expansive spaces, choose large plants like these remarkable palms as anchors, then layer in smaller plantings to infuse greenery throughout the room, with contrast in size and texture.

In a bright and spacious setting like a sunroom or loft, the licuala's majestic form gets a chance to shine. When choosing a location for these statement pieces, treat their foliage as a green canopy and situate the plants where people can view them from underneath, so the remarkable span of their leaves can be fully appreciated. If possible, place them near a window that can be opened during the warmer months; their fronds will sway captivatingly when caught by the breeze.

NINE

RULE BREAKERS

UNEXPECTED & UNFAMILIAR

INDOOR PLANTS

FOR INDOOR GARDENERS WHO ARE WILLING TO THINK outside the box, the botanical world offers endless opportunities. While we've curated most chapters in this book to highlight plants with similar attributes or design applications, the plants here were chosen for the opposite reason: they're all outliers. Thanks to an unusual form, atypical care requirements, or a tendency to be used in outdoor gardens, each one defies categorization within the world of houseplants.

A decidedly mixed bag in terms of scale and habit, this group provides a refreshing counterpoint to current houseplant trends that skew heavily toward tropical foliage favorites like ficus and monstera. Here you'll find woolly vines, cascading blooms, and ombré shrubs. Some—like the shade- and humidity-loving fernleaf cactus—have little in common with their relatives when it comes to care. Others, like feathery bamboo muhly grass, are familiar faces in outdoor landscapes that open up new design directions when invited inside. And still others, like the craggy-rooted climbing rock plant, were chosen simply for their beguiling strangeness. As a group, the specimens we're profiling here challenge traditional notions about what constitutes a houseplant.

While this chapter offers a wide range of unusual options, we see it as just the beginning of a conversation about what kinds of plants can be introduced to our living spaces. We hope it will encourage you to experiment and play with bringing new specimens home.

Argyreia nervosa

WOOLLY MORNING GLORY

THE EXPRESSIVE COMMON NAME "woolly morning glory" captures our favorite thing about this plant: its delightful texture. This tropical offers layer upon layer of visual interest, starting with its thick and fuzzy white vines. These vines support enormous heart-shaped leaves that combine the same soft, touchable texture with vivid color; the undersides are white, while the tops are an attention-grabbing chartreuse.

Its looks alone are a reason to bring *Argyreia nervosa* home, but there's much more to love. This vigorous plant is gratifying to watch while it grows, its vines spiraling and twining as they reach skyward. New leaves emerge pure white and fuzzy, throwing off corkscrew tendrils for a charming finishing touch.

Woolly morning glory is native to the Indian subcontinent, where it grows in rain forests, open woodlands, and even along roadsides— a testament to the adaptability that makes it suitable for use inside. Though it needs consistent warmth like many tropical houseplants, it can thrive in drier conditions than most tropicals. It will quickly and happily grow indoors year-round, but you can also move it to a covered porch during the summer months; just avoid letting it cling to any outdoor surfaces, so you can easily bring it back inside.

If you're looking for immediate impact, woolly morning glory is an extremely fast grower, offering lots of vertical interest in a short time frame. And it doesn't put out the damaging roots that many climbers produce; this means you can train it to grow on a built-in surface like an unheated pipe without worry. (It will also flourish on a trellis or stand-alone structure—such as the tripod shown opposite.) Its best asset, however, is its fantastically textural appearance. Its verdant presence has the potential to entirely transform an indoor space.

LIGHT • Full sun to bright indirect light.

WATER • Water when the soil becomes dry; do not overwater.

HUMIDITY • Appreciates humidity and an occasional misting but can thrive in dry indoor spaces.

SOIL • Well-draining potting mix.

FERTILIZER • Apply a balanced liquid fertilizer at half the manufacturer's recommended rate every two weeks during the growing season (spring to summer), tapering off to once a month in fall and ceasing in winter.

PESTS & DISEASE • Can be susceptible to spider mites and mealybugs.

SHOPPING • Look for this vine at nurseries that stock specialty annuals, or purchase seeds to grow your own. (It will grow quickly.)

PRUNING • Woolly morning glory grows up to 25 feet (7.5 m) in a single season, but can easily and harmlessly be pruned to a moderate size.

Muhlenbergia dumosa

BAMBOO MUHLY GRASS

WHILE GRASSES AREN'T COMMONLY USED as houseplants, we love this one as an indoor specimen. A departure from grasses with super-vertical silhouettes, bamboo muhly grass has a full, draping shape, and it adapts to the indoors better than most.

This fast-growing species is native to southern Arizona and northern Mexico, where it can reach a height of 6 feet (1.8 m) in the wild; it maxes out at around 4 feet (1.2 m) indoors. You've likely seen it used as an outdoor annual, but it will grow indefinitely as a houseplant—and that growth is truly stunning. Sprouting from a clump that's the perfect shape to nestle in a container, it has fine stems that develop a gracefully arched silhouette as they reach maturity. The clump expands quickly in size with proper care; to give your plant an extra boost, consider moving it outdoors during the warm summer months.

Bamboo muhly grass's overall look is best described as "fluffy," a captivating textural departure from most houseplants. Rich in movement, its form invokes the feeling that you've invited a piece of the landscape inside. It's a great alternative to an indoor tree, a verdant statement piece without a towering, heavy presence. If planted in a row of containers or a long trough, these grasses can also serve as a room divider—see pages 232–233. As unique as it is adaptable, this gorgeous grass has no trouble making itself at home.

LIGHT • Full sun; a window with bright direct light is ideal.

WATER • Water thoroughly once per week. Can tolerate some dryness, but grows more quickly with consistent watering.

HUMIDITY • Benefits from misting, but overall unfussy about humidity.

SOIL • Well-draining potting mix.

FERTILIZER • Apply a balanced liquid fertilizer at half the manufacturer's recommended rate every two weeks during the growing season (spring to summer), tapering to once a month in fall and ceasing in winter.

PESTS & DISEASE • Susceptible to mealybugs.

SHOPPING • Often stocked at garden centers offering specialty annuals, this fast-growing grass is found in 1- to 3-gallon (4 to 11 L) pots. The size of the clump will increase substantially in a single year.

PRUNING • Some stems will brown and die off as the plant ages; prune these away to prevent shedding.

PROPAGATION • As the grass clump grows larger, sections can be divided and repotted.

CLIMBING ROCK PLANT

LIGHT • Bright to moderate indirect light.

WATER • Keep the soil evenly moist but not saturated during periods of growth. Stop watering altogether if the plant becomes dormant (see below).

SOIL • Well-draining succulent mix.

FERTILIZER • Apply a balanced liquid fertilizer at half the manufacturer's recommended rate once a month during the growing season (spring to summer), tapering off in fall and ceasing in winter.

SHOPPING • *Stephania perrieri* grows very slowly; large specimens are twenty to thirty years old and commensurately expensive. Look for starter sizes at your local garden center; specialty growers will have older specimens. Buy what you can afford and enjoy the growth process!

POTTING • If you purchase a plant without a visible caudex, wait about a year for signs of growth. Once the root begins to swell, encourage growth by repotting with the shoulders of the root exposed. As the caudex grows, continue to gradually pull away soil to expose it.

GROWTH • Your plant may go dormant, dropping its leaves in autumn or early winter. Don't stress—dormancy is a way to gather energy for the next growing season. You should see new foliage develop as the days get longer. (Year-round growth is also healthy.)

THE CLIMBING ROCK PLANT, a vining native of Southeast Asia, is just one species in a large and diverse group known as caudiciforms. These unusual specimens possess a caudex: a large swollen root, basal stem, or trunk that becomes elevated above the surface of the soil.

The caudex develops differently on each plant—it may begin with a smooth texture, like a potato, and can evolve to a surface covered in spikes and bumps, a tuberous silhouette, or a geometric, cracked-earth patterning. In the case of the climbing rock plant, it first emerges small and smooth, expanding and developing a furrowed texture over time.

The formation of the caudex makes this slow-growing specimen an outlandish delight. Because a mature caudex can take decades to develop, caudiciforms are prized by collectors, particularly in Japan and in the western United States. Turn to pages 238–239 to see extraordinary caudex specimens at one of our favorite growers, Landcraft Environments.

Don't despair if your caudex isn't mature yet: a climbing rock plant's foliage is beguiling in its own right. The slender vines have the curling and delicate texture of maidenhair fern stems. Each one sprouts platelike leaves, which can be heart-shaped or mostly round. The high-contrast pairing of these two seemingly separate elements—tropical foliage perched atop craggy caudex—is an exotic outlier among vining species.

For an added layer of interest, train the dainty vines to grow on a structure. Try a wire hoop (shown opposite) or obelisk if you'd like a defined form, or use a simple tripod to encourage more natural-looking growth. No matter the shape, a structure gives your vine a place to call home in the decades ahead. It's a long-term commitment worth making.

Breynia disticha 'Roseo Picta'

PINK SNOWBUSH

DON'T BE FOOLED by its frosty common name, the snowbush is a tropical stunner. Native to the South Pacific, it was first popularized in the United States as an outdoor shrub or hedge in the temperate climes of Florida and California. In recent years, however, its intriguing coloration and shape have helped it gain traction as an indoor plant.

You can find a host of different tricolor houseplants, but the snowbush is unique in the way color is distributed across its foliage. While most plants have individual tricolor leaves, the motif is spread across the leaves of this plant. Green-and-white mottling gives it a snow-dusted look, which is topped off by a kiss of hot pink at the tip of each stem. The resulting layered ombré effect is stunning as an addition to interior spaces filled with lots of solid greenery.

Though its coloring alone would be enough to attract many admirers, the snowbush also boasts a superlative shape. Its rounded alternate leaves perch atop slender stems for a delicate, fluttery feel akin to a maidenhair fern (page 141) or a scaled-down ficus triangularis (page 210). This dainty and tidily arranged foliage is even more striking when juxtaposed with the plant's bushy overall silhouette.

While it won't grow as large as, say, an indoor tree, the snowbush will be a substantial and instantly gratifying presence in your home. Most nurseries offer 2-foot-tall (0.6 m) specimens, which fill in quickly with proper care. With a mature size of 4 feet (1.2 m) tall and wide, it's perfectly poised to round out a space with lots of vibrant color.

LIGHT • Provide ample bright indirect light; lack of light can dull the foliage's color.

WATER • Keep the soil consistently moist; a watering globe, self-watering pot, or drip feeder can help maintain moisture. If the plant becomes too dry, recovery can be difficult.

HUMIDITY • Requires high ambient humidity.

SOIL • Rich potting mix with good water retention.

FERTILIZER • In the growing season (spring to fall), feed with a balanced liquid fertilizer every two weeks at half the manufacturer's recommended rate. Plants may rest in winter, but if they are still growing, fertilize once a month.

PESTS & DISEASE • Can be susceptible to mealybugs and scale. Both are more likely to occur if conditions are too dry.

SHOPPING • This is sometimes sold as *Breynia nivosa*. In addition to tricolor 'Roseo Picta', you can find plants with white-and-green or yellow-and-green variegations.

POTTING • *B. disticha* prefers cramped roots and will have stronger coloration when not potted in excess soil. Repot every few years.

PRUNING • Prune as needed to maintain your desired shape.

PROPAGATION • Can be propagated with stem cuttings in soil.

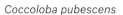
Coccoloba pubescens

GRANDLEAF SEAGRAPE

AS YOU MAY HAVE GUESSED from its common name, the leaves are the most outstanding feature of this tropical tree. Different *Coccoloba* species have a wide variety of leaf sizes, from modest (around 5 inches/13 cm) to spectacularly grand. While *C. pubescens* doesn't boast the largest leaves in the group, its foliage is still quite impressive: a single leaf can reach up to 3 feet (91 cm) in diameter. It's a common sight along Caribbean coasts but relatively unknown in the houseplant world. A whimsical oddity, it introduces an exciting new shape to the category of large upright houseplants.

Though most notable for their scale, *C. pubescens* leaves have lots of additional charm. They're stiff and finely veined, with greenish tops, ruffled edges, and undersides that vary in color from yellow to burnished red depending on light exposure and temperature. Their rugged texture of raised bumps and prominent veins is surprisingly reminiscent of a begonia (pages 93–99), though the two plants exist on opposite ends of the size spectrum. Small to midsize *C. pubescens* plants can benefit from additional support as their massive leaves grow; try pairing your tree with a simple bamboo pole to help it stay upright.

In the wild, grandleaf seagrapes can reach up to 78 feet (24 m) tall, but they grow relatively slowly and can easily be pruned to a manageable size indoors. Though upright and minimally branching overall, your tree will develop lots of character as it matures, taking on an increasingly irregular form. The leaves themselves grow outward in layers, producing a series of plateaus. This striated effect captures your gaze when you enter a room, inviting a closer look at this plant's fantastic foliage.

LIGHT • Bright indirect light. Low-light conditions can cause sparse leaves, thin stems, or the tendency to lean toward a light source.

WATER • Keep the soil consistently moist, but do not leave in standing water. Weekly watering is usually sufficient.

HUMIDITY • Needs humidity to thrive.

SOIL • Well-draining potting mix amended with organic matter, sand, and orchid bark for added nutrition and drainage.

FERTILIZER • Apply a slow-release granular indoor fertilizer every four to six months. Follow the manufacturer's instructions for rates and application. If the plant shows acute nutrient distress (leaf drop and discoloration) between granular feedings, sparingly apply a balanced liquid fertilizer every third watering until distress abates.

Selenicereus chrysocardium

FERNLEAF CACTUS

THE COMMON NAME "FERNLEAF CACTUS" may bring to mind a spiky and sun-loving desert denizen, but this plant is an entirely different beast. Though it is a member of the cactus family, it grows as an epiphyte in the jungles of Mexico, where it makes its home on rocks and trees in the humid understory. Part fern, part succulent, and all character, it's in a houseplant category of its own.

Reminiscent of a fern in overall silhouette but much easier to care for, *Selenicereus chrysocardium* boasts heavily lobed leaves with a fleshy, succulent-like texture. (They're spineless—so no need to worry about prickly mishaps!) This plant is a vigorous grower, its undulating arms taking on surprising shapes as they amble outward to a mature size of up to 6 feet (1.8 m) wide. While its foliage is endearingly eccentric, its blooms are also exceptional. They're slow to emerge, but they reward patience with their bright white hue and spectacular scale, reaching up to 12 inches (30 cm) across.

Make the most of your fernleaf cactus's ample character by showcasing it where it can stretch out. The far-reaching leaves shine when sprawling from a hanging basket, the top of a cabinet, or a bookshelf. If you live in a place with humid summers, treat your plant to a vacation in a shady outdoor space while the weather is warm; it will appreciate the return to its jungle roots.

LIGHT • Bright indirect light. Can tolerate morning sun with afternoon shade.

WATER • Let the soil dry between waterings. Try a weekly or biweekly schedule in summer, reducing frequency in winter.

HUMIDITY • Benefits from humidity.

SOIL • Well-draining potting mix amended with organic matter and orchid bark or other aggregates for added drainage, nutrition, and structure.

FERTILIZER • Feed sparingly with a low-nitrogen liquid fertilizer once a month at half the manufacturer's recommended rate or less. Switch to a high phosphorus-potassium fertilizer as buds develop. Fernleaf cacti need lots of light if being fed; plants in low-light conditions should receive even less supplemental fertilizing. Do not feed in winter.

POTTING • Do not repot frequently; will bloom best when slightly pot-bound.

MEDINILLA

THREE OF THIS PLANT'S COMMON NAMES—"pink lantern plant," "rose grape," and "Malaysian orchid"—reveal much about the aesthetic charms of *Medinilla magnifica*. This tropical shrub possesses extraordinarily beautiful blooms that make comparisons to orchids well deserved. It outshines the orchid, however, thanks to its large scale, hardiness, and showy foliage.

Abundant and dramatic, *M. magnifica*'s blooms first emerge as tight, pale pink clusters, which gradually elongate into graceful, downward-arching cascades known as panicles. As the flowers mature, they change from light pink to bright pink to fuchsia, often accented with touches of violet, before ripening into a cluster of berries. A single panicle can reach 18 inches (45 cm) long, a scale that's noteworthy among blooming houseplants. Deep green leaves with heavy veining provide a moody backdrop for these stunning blooms. Best of all, this sturdy shrub reblooms reliably, so you can enjoy fresh and long-lasting flowers without the fuss that an orchid requires.

Native to the Philippines, *M. magnifica* grows in the wild as an epiphyte, perching on trees in tropical forests. You'll likely find it for use as a houseplant in the form of an upright shrub. It can reach 4 to 6 feet (1.2 to 1.8 m) tall at maturity, but don't worry about it outgrowing your space; it's a moderate grower and can be pruned to maintain your desired scale. (Keep in mind that larger plants will produce more flowers.) Pleasantly undemanding and exceptionally rewarding, it's the perfect statement piece for an entryway or any room that needs a splash of color.

LIGHT • Bright light; can tolerate indirect light but should not be exposed to full afternoon sun. Browning at the leaf tips can indicate too much sun, or lack of humidity if the plant receives only indirect light.

WATER • During the growing season, water when the top 2 inches (5 cm) of soil become dry. Reduce watering frequency outside the growing season, but never let the soil dry out completely.

HUMIDITY • Benefits from humidity and misting.

SOIL • 50/50 mix of potting mix and orchid mix.

FERTILIZER • In the growing season (spring to fall), feed with an orchid-specific fertilizer or a fertilizer high in phosphorous every two weeks. When no longer flowering, stop fertilizing.

SHOPPING • Buy this plant if you see it; availability is inconsistent. Expect a plant in a 6- to 8-inch (15 to 20 cm) pot to have one or two blooms; plants in 10- to 12-inch (25 to 30 cm) pots can have six or more.

PRUNING • If your plant becomes too large, you can shape it to maintain your desired size. Prune only after flowering.

AN INDOOR MEADOW

Because the specimens in this chapter push the boundaries of what can be a houseplant, they're ideal for experimenting with how greenery can function as a decorative element. This trio of bamboo muhly grass planters, for example, creates the curious and immersive effect of sitting in a field indoors. Perched on a sideboard, the grasses form a feathery canopy, allowing you to play with height in a way that's less overt than if you'd used a broad-leaved specimen like, say, a licuala (page 202). In larger rooms, this style of repetition is perfect for creating an organic dividing wall that's rich in textural intrigue.

The curvy planters we chose for these grasses give the display additional presence. While the texture of the vessels is quite rugged, their shapes keep them from feeling too hefty; the refined, narrow bases lift their visual weight and subtly echo the silhouettes of the plants. Their wide mouths also serve a practical purpose, giving the grass lots of horizontal space for root growth at the soil line, so each planting will become fuller over time.

LANDCRAFT ENVIRONMENTS & GARDEN FOUNDATION

MATTITUCK, NEW YORK

For those who love exotic plants, the greenhouses and gardens of Landcraft are a place like no other. On Long Island's North Fork, Dennis Schrader and Bill Smith cultivate everything from tropical trees to monstrous cane begonias to desert-dwelling caudiciforms. Now they've opened their botanical wonderland to the public for the first time, so they can help grow the next generation of gardeners.

Landcraft started in 1982 as a garden design business, rooted in Dennis's lifelong love of plants and Bill's fine-art background. Dennis says, "We designed for some large estates but also created lots of container gardens. We changed out the containers four or five times a year; one season we'd plant tropical fruit trees, another we might plug the drainage holes and create water gardens. It was a lot of fun, but we could never find enough unusual plants to keep spicing things up."

Their nursery, Landcraft Environments, was born of a need for exotic plants to fill those containers season after season. "We would go through seed catalogs and see all these amazing plants that we couldn't get. So we started growing them for ourselves," Dennis explains. "Along the way, I realized that I liked the growing better. So we decided to buy our farm in 1992."

When they purchased the property, their 1840s farmhouse was "surrounded by poison ivy," its 17 acres (7 ha) of land depleted by corn and potato farming. Dennis and Bill spent the first year growing cover crops to remediate the soil. Since then, they've

---

Dennis and Bill's personal collection of spectacular plant specimens, gathered in its winter storage location. These plants will move back into the gardens during the summer months.

transformed the landscape with formal gardens, native plant meadows, and various houses where they grow an astounding 1,600 species of plants for sale. "The houses," Dennis says, "are designed for different climates, from shady and humid to sunny and arid. Specialized growers run out screaming when they see it, but for us it has to be interesting."

While their greenhouses re-create climates from across the globe, Landcraft has its own microclimate. Sandwiched between Peconic Bay and Long Island Sound, the gardens enjoy a long, moderate growing season. "Sometimes we don't get a frost until December or January," Dennis says. "Cutchogue, about two blocks away, is the sunniest place in the state." The mild climate allows Dennis and Bill to blur the line between indoors and out, challenging traditional ideas about houseplants. "You can treat tropicals as annuals outside, or just move them outdoors during the warmer months," Dennis says. "I started by putting my houseplants out for the summer. It surprised people, but I wondered why we don't do this all the time."

Among the plants that move in and out through the seasons are Dennis's collection of around 350 caudiciforms: plants characterized by an enormous caudex (see more on page 222). These otherworldly specimens fascinate him because "so many plants have a caudex in their genus. Begonias, geraniums, gloxinias, and African violets all have a caudex type." He also loves these peculiar plants for their unusual growth cycles; many go dormant for months before bursting to life. He cites *Pseudobombax ellipticum*—a tree with a turtle shell–shaped caudex—as a prime example. "The *Pseudobombax* blooming is a harbinger of spring. In February, the dead of winter, it comes out of dormancy with giant white flowers." (Turn to page 238 to see this remarkable specimen.) Another new

ABOVE: Dennis (left) and Bill surrounded by tropicals, succulents, and cascades of Spanish moss in the collection house. OPPOSITE, CLOCKWISE FROM TOP LEFT: The rugged trunk of a thaumatophyllum; a cluster of fruit from a variegated banana (*Musa × paradisiaca* 'Ae Ae'); the myrtle topiary production area, including the cart where each plant is shaped.

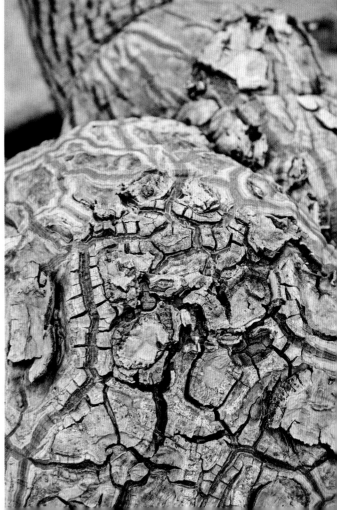

favorite is *Welwitschia mirabilis*, a Namibian desert native that after months of dormancy sprouts just two curly, rambling leaves. It can live for hundreds of years.

Landcraft's love affair with caudiciforms led to a one-of-a-kind project at the Bronx Zoo: over the course of two years, they imported and grew a huge number of exotic specimens for a new lemur exhibit. After installation, the lemurs showed their appreciation by reaching through their enclosure, pulling the trees in, and eating them all.

While the lemur exhibit may be the most unusual project in their history, Dennis and Bill's most extraordinary work is their own property, which opened to the public as the Landcraft Garden Foundation in 2021. Visitors can explore a spectacular landscape of lushly planted spaces, including a subterranean ruin and a "tiki" hut that houses their orchid collection, plus programs including yoga classes, art installations, and illustration workshops. Up next? A meditation labyrinth centered by ammonite-studded stone chairs. Dennis says, "We went from soft opening to full opening very quickly! It's a lot of work, but a great team supports us: our gardeners, board, art and education committees, and volunteers."

OPPOSITE, TOP: High-color begonia and coleus mother plants used for production. Notice the towering cane begonias in the foreground. OPPOSITE, BOTTOM: *Pseudobombax ellipticum*, entering its early winter dormancy; and a closer look at its deeply fissured caudex. ABOVE: Dennis recommends displaying caudiciforms, like this *Hydnophytum moseleyanum*, alone: "Treat them as living sculptures. Showcase their unique shapes in a bonsai-type pot or add a layer of gravel atop the soil to highlight their gigantic roots."

Dennis and Bill have big plans for the years ahead, including a conservatory to house their collection and host events throughout the winter. "Our long-term mission is inspiring and educating new generations of gardeners," Dennis says. To that end, they've established a yearlong mentoring program, described as a "finishing school" for horticulturists. "It's designed for someone who just finished a program at a place like Longwood or the New York Botanical Garden and isn't sure what they want to do. Students will do hands-on work in the greenhouse, the wholesale business, the garden, and with board members and landscape architects. It rounds out their education with a chance to work in the real world—including not-so-glamorous parts like loading plant carts in the rain."

Though their future programming centers on real-world experience, Dennis and Bill don't have a narrow view of what horticulture can be. Inspired by their own backgrounds in art and design, they've assembled a remarkably diverse and creative team to join them in growing the foundation, including chefs, writers, architects, and even a poet who pens their newsletters. "We want to get at the intersection of art and horticulture in an intentional way," Dennis says. "The impetus for all of our work is to ensure that the garden lives on beyond us."

ABOVE: A pair of *Alcantarea odorata*; note the tall, arching inflorescence coming from the left plant. OPPOSITE: Bill and Dennis's extensive orchid collection.

FOLLOWING PAGES: The Landcraft Garden Foundation's public spaces include paths that wander through both formal and meadow-inspired gardens. This is a transition point between those environments, on an early-winter morning.

GLOSSARY

Aggregate. A material (in this context, used to create a potting blend) composed of a blend of particles, which may be of a single type or mixed.

Annual. A plant that grows, flowers, produces seed, and dies within one year and does not return the next.

Aphid. A sucking insect that can come in many colors; it feeds on tender new growth and reproduces at a phenomenal rate.

Areola (areole). An area on a cactus from which spines or hairs emerge.

Botrytis. Gray mold that thrives in cool, damp environments and is most often found growing on fruit and flowers that remain wet overnight.

Bract. A leaflike structure found above the leaves of a plant, usually just below a flower bud, stalk, or inflorescence.

Cachepot. A decorative container without drainage holes.

Caudex. A large swollen root, basal stem, or trunk that becomes elevated above the surface of the soil.

Caudiciform. A plant that possesses a caudex, or swollen aboveground root or stem.

Chlorophyll. A compound responsible for the green pigment of plants and algae, essential in the process of photosynthesis.

Cladode. A fleshy paddle that serves as a leaf.

Cladophyll. A flattened branch that functions as a leaf.

Clonal propagation. A method of propagation that results in the exact same plant as the one being propagated.

Corm. A tiny ovate food storage structure that multiplies in a clump below the stem.

Dibber. A hand tool, often with a wooden handle and metal point, used to make holes in soil for planting seeds or seedlings.

Dissected. A foliage descriptor that indicates deeply indented margins dividing a single leaf.

Epiphyte. A nonparasitic plant that, in its native habitats, lives on other plants or rocks and derives nutrients from air and water.

Fenestration. A hole that develops in a once-solid leaf.

Fiddlehead. A newly emerged fern frond in a tightly coiled shape.

Frass. Tiny specks of waste product produced by insects.

Frond. Botanical term for a fern's leaf.

Fungus gnat. A tiny black fly that is generally harmless but whose larvae (maggots) can sometimes damage plant roots.

Glaucous. A descriptor that indicates a pale gray-green color, or bluish powdery layer on leaves or fruit.

Guttation. The process by which water seeps out of a plant's leaf tips or edges.

Habit. The overall size, shape, and form inherent to a particular plant.

Honeydew. Insect secretion on the plant surface that can lead to sooty mold.

Inflorescence. A plant's complete flower head, including stems, stalks, bracts, and flowers.

Internode. The space between leaves or buds.

Mealybug. A round, soft-bodied insect covered in white, waxy "fluff" that thrives in warm, moist environments and clusters along stems, under leaves, and along leaf veins. Mealybugs produce honeydew, a source of sooty mold.

Node. The point of growth on a plant (the origin of a bud, branch, or petiole).

NPK value. A set of numbers that expresses the percentage by volume of nitrogen, phosphorus, and potassium respectively in a fertilizer formulation.

Nutrient rich. Descriptor for soil or soilless potting mix that provides macro- and micronutrients to a plant, or a component that manages the release of such nutrients when added. For example, compost is very nutrient rich.

Nyctinastic. Referring to plants with leaves that open and close each day in a slow-motion gesture that resembles hands being brought together in prayer.

Oedema (edema). A hard, lumpy growth on the underside of a leaf that is caused by too much water and not enough light.

Palmate. A leaf shape featuring lobes that radiate from a central point, like an open hand.

Panicle. A flower head composed of many smaller branches, each containing more than one flower.

Peduncle. A stalk or stem bearing flowers.

Petiole. A stalk or stem bearing leaves.

Photosynthesis. The process by which plants capture and convert light energy into usable energy.

Porous. Descriptor for a potting mix with lots of space for root growth, gas exchange, and water movement.

Rhizomes. A network of modified stems that usually grows horizontally below the surface of the soil. Rhizomes may also grow above the soil as rhizomatous feet, as seen in some footed fern species (see pages 130 and 134).

Rot. Plant tissue that has become soft, brown, and mushy; caused by many pathogens.

Scale. Round, soft-bodied insects that cover themselves with waxy brown shells as adults and tend to cluster along stems, under leaves, and along leaf veins. They produce honeydew, a source of sooty mold.

Sooty mold. Unsightly black fungus that grows on honeydew (the sweet excrement of insects) and obstructs light from reaching plants' leaves.

Spider mite. An almost microscopic pest that feeds on the underside of the leaf, causing stippling or a silver to bronze sheen on foliage.

Spores. Tiny dark dots on the underside of the frond; a fern's method of reproduction.

Sport. Spontaneous mutation that occurs as new plants grow.

Stomas. Microscopic pores that allow a plant to expel gas and water vapor, which is essential to the photosynthesis process.

Substrate. The soil or any substance on which a plant lives.

Terrestrial. A plant that grows on land, rather than in water or suspended on rocks and trees.

Transpiration. The process by which plants absorb, circulate, and release water.

Trifoliate. Referring to a leaf that is divided into three leaflets.

Umbel. A form of flower cluster where stalks of similar lengths are suspended from a central point on a stem, forming a flat plane. Typical of the *Hoya* genus.

Whitefly. A tiny white flying, sucking insect that clusters under leaves and produces honeydew, which can lead to sooty mold.

RESOURCES

Favorite Botanical Gardens

FAIRCHILD TROPICAL BOTANIC GARDEN
Coral Gables, Florida

Nestled along southern Florida's Biscayne Bay, this garden was named for David Fairchild. A renowned plant explorer, Fairchild was responsible for the establishment of the Office of Foreign Seed and Plant Introduction at the US Department of Agriculture; many of the plants that he collected still grow in his namesake garden today. Myriad licualas, rare palms, cycads, and mature anthuriums dot the misty understory of the rain forest surrounding the glasshouse complex. Look for beautiful cane and rhizomatous begonia specimens in the Tropical Plant Conservatory and Rare Plant House, alongside mature philodendrons, ferns, mosses, and rare anthuriums. The International Aroid Society (see page 249) hosts an annual show and plant sale here each February.

FOSTER BOTANICAL GARDEN
Honolulu, Hawaii

Tucked into the middle of busy downtown Honolulu, Foster is a smaller garden at just 14 acres (5.6 ha). It's home, however, to an awe-inspiring array of old-growth tropical trees. Towering rainbow eucalyptus and traveler's palms, among others, rise from a sea of plush grass. A smaller conservatory houses a riotous tangle of tropical plants and an extensive orchid collection.

GARFIELD PARK CONSERVATORY
Chicago, Illinois

A beautiful garden and glasshouse in the Chicago Park District, the Garfield Park Conservatory has a suggested donation model for entry and a focus on community-centric educational programming. Housing one of the most remarkable collections in the United States, the Fern Room alone is worth the trip. As you wander through the world of mosses and epiphytic footed ferns that creep along its craggy rock walls, look for one of our favorite species: the skeleton fork fern.

HORTUS BOTANICUS
Amsterdam, the Netherlands

Founded in 1638 by the city of Amsterdam, the Hortus is one of the oldest botanic gardens in the world. It started as a physic garden for medicinal herbs, many of which are still grown there today. The exterior gardens surround a Palm House that boasts giant licuala specimens, and the garden's three-climate greenhouse was designed with separate zones to support plants from the tropics, the desert, and the subtropics. The Desert Room is a stunning display, with its bright walls offsetting graphic succulents and cacti in an array of hues and textures.

THE HUNTINGTON LIBRARY, ART MUSEUM, AND BOTANICAL GARDENS
San Marino, California

This largely outdoor destination is both a functional research garden and home to some of the most extensive plant collections in the United States. The Huntington features an incredible in-ground Jungle Garden and Palm Garden, and the Desert Garden, one of the oldest and largest outdoor collections of succulents and cacti in the world, is unmissable; its stunning agave specimens and towering yucca will stop you in your tracks. A tip for those building their own plant collections: the Huntington releases plant introductions each year, offering propagated seedlings and rooted cuttings of new and rare succulents that can be ordered at very accessible price points via an annual catalog.

JARDÍN BOTÁNICO DEL BOSQUE DE CHAPULTEPEC
Mexico City, Mexico

You'll find this modestly sized, largely outdoor botanical garden tucked inside the massive Bosque de Chapultepec, a forested park in the heart of Mexico City. The garden features an impressive in-ground agave and opuntia planting in a surreal wooded setting and offers a rare chance to see single species both en masse and alongside one another. The greenhouse holds an extensive orchid collection as well as rambling fern cacti, cycads, and aroids, all nested in alcoves that feature stunning stained glass and tile work.

KEW GARDENS
London, England

A UNESCO World Heritage Site, Kew is the world's largest botanical garden at 330 acres (132 ha). The land that now houses its gardens was the site of royal residences beginning in 1299; it became a national botanic garden in 1840, largely due to the work of the Royal Horticultural Society. The nineteenth-century Palm House and Temperate House are stunning Victorian glasshouses filled with some of the world's rarest plants. In the Palm House, climb the circular stairs to a catwalk suspended around the central nave and peer into the massive fronds from above. Outdoors, you'll find both manicured gardens and ambling pleasure grounds, boasting a treetop walkway, several trees over 250 years old, and endless paths through forests and meadows. Kew Gardens remains one of the foremost botanical research and education institutions in the world.

LONGWOOD GARDENS
Kennett Square, Pennsylvania

A short drive from the Terrain flagship in Glen Mills, this storied garden speaks to the deep horticultural roots of the Philadelphia area. Longwood offers acres of outdoor garden paths surrounding the Conservatory, a massive glasshouse filled with highly layered display gardens. Famed Brazilian landscape designer, artist, and philodendron collector Roberto Burle Marx designed the tropical Cascade Garden in the late 1980s. One of his last completed works before his death, it opened in 1994 and is now the only existing Burle Marx garden in North America. The Conservatory overlooks the Main Fountain Gardens, next to which you'll find the historic Rose Garden—recently redesigned (as part of a broader reimagining at Longwood) by our friend, former Terrain buyer, and horticultural editor for this book, Kerry Ann McLean.

MORRIS ARBORETUM
Philadelphia, Pennsylvania

This northwest Philadelphia destination is run by the University of Pennsylvania, which uses the arboretum for research focused on the conservation of plants and ecosystems. Morris is set on just shy of 100 acres (40 ha), dappled with old-growth trees, meadows, and gardens. Tucked into the property, you'll find a tiny gem: the Dorrance H. Hamilton Fernery, which is North America's only remaining freestanding Victorian fernery. A product of the Victorian fern obsession, this octagonal, slightly sunken glasshouse was originally home to over five hundred varieties of ferns and mosses. It was restored in the early 1990s with the support of the late Mrs. Hamilton, one of the region's strongest proponents of horticulture.

NEW YORK BOTANICAL GARDEN
Bronx, New York

Sharing Bronx Park with the Bronx Zoo, NYBG is the largest botanic garden in the United States and operates one of the world's most extensive plant research and conservation programs. Its indoor collection is housed in the Enid A. Haupt Conservatory, completed in 1902 and modeled after the Palm House at Kew. The conservatory is home to outstanding collections of palms, aroids, and ferns, as well as tropical flowering plants. NYBG offers incredible access to horticultural experts; it answers houseplant care questions via social media as part of its Plant Doctor series, and its library operates a plant information office specifically for answering home gardening questions. In recent years, NYBG has increasingly explored plants and intersectionality through exhibitions and programs that seek to center Indigenous, Black, and brown voices.

QUEEN SIRIKIT BOTANIC GARDEN
Chiang Mai, Thailand

Take the winding road to this magical garden through the jungle-covered mountains above Chiang Mai; along the way, you'll spot massive mature *Epipremnum* climbing ancient ficus trees and shady mountainsides blanketed in tree ferns. The garden itself features a canopy walk with endless trails in the jungle below, as well as ten glasshouses filled with collections ranging from arid to tropical. The Palm House holds a collection of awe-inspiring giant fan palm species, with calatheas, aroids, and other tropicals growing below. Plan to spend a whole day; you'll need it to explore collections that include maidenhair ferns, cacti, carnivorous plants, and more.

Plant Societies and Clubs

Plant societies and clubs are great places to meet like-minded plant lovers or find a mentor if you're seeking more knowledge about a particular area of interest. Annual membership dues are typically affordable, and most societies regularly release a journal or newsletter. These groups foster conversation around plant care, identification, propagation, and taxonomy, as well as the trade of seeds, cuttings, and small plants. If there isn't a chapter local to you, consider starting one!

THE INTERNATIONAL AROID SOCIETY
aroid.org

THE AMERICAN BEGONIA SOCIETY
begonias.org

THE NATIONAL BEGONIA SOCIETY
national-begonia-society.co.uk

THE ASSOCIATION OF AUSTRALIAN BEGONIA SOCIETIES
begoniaaustralis.wordpress.com

CACTUS & SUCCULENT SOCIETY OF AMERICA
cactusandsucculentsociety.org

PHILADELPHIA CACTUS & SUCCULENT SOCIETY
philacactus.org

TUCSON CACTUS & SUCCULENT SOCIETY
tcss.wildapricot.org

AMERICAN FERN SOCIETY
amerfernsoc.org

DELAWARE VALLEY FERN & WILDFLOWER SOCIETY
dvfws.org

THE GESNERIAD SOCIETY
gesneriadsociety.org

INTERNATIONAL HOYA ASSOCIATION
international-hoya.org

Recommended Reading

Around the World in 80 Plants by Jonathan Drori

The Earth in Her Hands by Jennifer Jewell

Finland Living Design by Elizabeth Gaynor

The Gardens of Roberto Burle Marx by Sima Eliovson

Greenworks by Judith Handelsman

Herbarium by Barbara M. Thiers

The House Plant Expert by Dr. D. G. Hessayon

Living with Plants by William S. Hawkey

Roberto Burle Marx: The Lyrical Landscape by Marta Iris Montero

Terence Conran's Decorating with Plants by Susan Conder

The Treasury of Houseplants by Rob Herwig and Margot Schubert

ACKNOWLEDGMENTS

AS IS OFTEN THE CASE in the plant community, this project was brought to life by the kindness and collaborative spirit of a small and incredibly talented group of friends and colleagues, to whom I owe a debt of gratitude, and without whom I would have been lost.

To Lacey Soslow, for advocating for this idea from the start and believing in this book, and for all the brainstorming, pep talks, friendship, and support throughout this process and over the past thirteen years.

To Caroline Lees, our most gracious writer and former Terrain brand voice, I'm forever grateful for and humbled by your patience, talent, and organization. Thank you for giving my thoughts structure and for bringing this book to life.

To Kerry Ann McLean, our horticulture writer and editor, Terrain plant team alum, and my forever mentor and friend. Your careful attention and passion for horticultural education and accessibility are so present in this book. Thank you for keeping me true and for your ceaseless, kind teaching.

To Kate Jordan, for bringing the vision for this book to life through your incredible images, for offering such joy and commitment to this project, for our grower road trip adventures, and for all the levity. Making this book with you was such a pleasure. And also to photographer Jamie Griffin for her gorgeous images at Harmony.

To Matt Muscarella, for styling every photo (and me!) and bringing your magic to this book, for the generous gift of your time and attention, for seeing me as few are able, and for always leading with empathy. I'm so grateful to have had this chance to create something lasting together. I could not have done it without you.

To Erika Boal, for your constant collaboration, but more so for showing up always and helping me find both perspective and my voice throughout this project.

To my editor, Bridget Monroe Itkin, for your kindness and patience, insight, and willingness to seriously engage with my every question. I so appreciate your deeply logical brain and total knack for the gentle nudge. Your critical partnership in shaping this book has been everything.

To Lia Ronnen and everyone at Artisan whose talent, expertise, and partnership made this book possible, including Sibylle Kazeroid, Paula Brisco, Suet Chong, Jane Treuhaft, Toni Tajima, Barbara Peragine, Nancy Murray, Donna G. Brown, Erica Huang, Allison McGeehon, Theresa Collier, Amy Michelson, and Fiona Winch. And to our agent, Judy Linden at Stonesong.

To Beth Smith and Greg Lehmkuhl for this opportunity and their unwavering support and belief in this book, and to everyone in our URBN and Terrain family, past and present—Richard and Meg Hayne, Tricia Smith, Matt Poarch, Melissa Bartley, Cat Boggs, Danielle Palencar, Diane Stulb, Megan Parry, Ashley Fossile, Lake Muir, and Steve Hensley—for bringing the Terrain brand to life. And to both the AnthroLiving and Urban Outfitters Home teams for some of the lovely furniture we used in photo styling.

To the many folks who gave operational support; loaned, hoarded, hauled, or tallied plants; or helped to keep (most) everything alive: Jessica Mercurio, Meghan Peters, Julie Czeck, Larry Bodhuin, Rebecca Costill, Kevin Boal, and the rest of the team at Terrain at Styer's. And to the rest of my Terrain plant team: Erin Sweeney, Kate Rath, Kelly Martin, Meredith Greene, Tracy Smith, Rachel Tomapat, and Ren He, thank you for your grace and the support to make this book happen.

To Michelle and George Garrambone at G & M Tropicals, as well as Jean Beck, for your tireless and sometimes heroic help in finding so many of the beautiful specimens featured here, and for your continued support of Terrain and me. And to Andrew Bunting and Dan Scott at the Pennsylvania Horticultural Society for the loan of their spectacular *Polypodium*.

To everyone who opened your beautiful homes as photo-shoot locations: Nicole Cole at Vestige Home, Kristal Hill, Todd Vladyka at Todd Judd Studio, Ashley Hannan, Lacey Soslow and Michelle Landry, and Matt Muscarella. And to Lindsey Scannapieco, Jackie Rush, Liz Maillie, Michael Ferreri, and the rest of the incredible family at BOK and Scout, for your consistent love and support and the chance to shoot in such a special space.

To my grower friends, old and new, who invited us into their spaces and shared their stories: Enid Offolter at NSE Tropicals; Deb Cox and Robin Jordan at Harmony Foliage; Matt, Kathy, and Ray Roberts and Logan VanderMaas at Central Florida Ferns & Foliage; Sid, Regina, and Paula Gardino at Gardino Nursery; and Dennis Schrader and Bill Smith at Landcraft Environments & Garden Foundation.

To my partner, Wen Blankenship, my creative center and perpetual collaborator, thank you for the gift of your talent in the botanical illustration, and for celebrating the magic in the details with me. Your love, steady care, and constant support (and commitment to keeping me caffeinated) were the only things that made this project possible. I cannot thank you enough for the myriad sacrifices and every big and small way you show up for me.

And to my mom, who pointed me to nature and taught me to celebrate each new sign of growth. Your plants are always healthier than mine, but you still ask for plant advice every time we talk. I cherish our habitual walks through your beautiful gardens at every visit. I am so grateful for you and your love.

INDEX

MELISSA LOWRIE is the divisional merchandise manager of plants and garden for Terrain. An industry leader with over twenty-five years of experience in the home and garden space, Lowrie got her start at Waterloo Gardens, a family-owned garden center in Chester County, Pennsylvania. She joined the Terrain team at its launch in 2008, and worked as a buyer, floral designer, and photo stylist for the brand prior to taking on her current role. She lives with her partner, artist and designer Wen Blankenship, and their two spotted pups, Jasper and Ru, in Philadelphia's Germantown neighborhood.

TERRAIN, a home and garden lifestyle brand under the URBN brand family, was founded in 2008 on the site of a hundred-year-old nursery in Glen Mills, Pennsylvania. The brand has now grown to include seven stores across the country, with a new location opening in Doylestown, Pennsylvania, in early 2023. Terrain has been featured on *Today* and CBS's *Sunday Morning* as well as in the *New York Times*, the *Wall Street Journal*, *Vanity Fair*, *Vogue*, *Martha Stewart Living*, *Elle Decor*, and *InStyle*. Their first book, *Terrain: Ideas and Inspiration for Decorating the Home and Garden*, was published in 2018.